Copyright Infringement

Other Books of Related Interest

Opposing Viewpoints Series

Civil Liberties

Cybercrime

Juvenile Crime

At Issue Series

Are Books Becoming Extinct?

Are Textbooks Biased?

Digitized Textbooks

Identity Theft

Policing the Internet

Current Controversies Series

E-books

The Global Impact of Social Media

Media Ethics

"Congress shall make no law ... abridging the freedom of speech, or of the press."

First Amendment to the US Constitution

The basic foundation of our democracy is the First Amendment guarantee of freedom of expression. The Opposing Viewpoints Series is dedicated to the concept of this basic freedom and the idea that it is more important to practice it than to enshrine it.

Copyright Infringement

Carol Ullmann and Lynn M. Zott, Book Editors

GREENHAVEN PRESS
A part of Gale, Cengage Learning

GALE
CENGAGE Learning·

Detroit • New York • San Francisco • New Haven, Conn • Waterville, Maine • London

Elizabeth Des Chenes, *Director, Content Strategy*
Cynthia Sanner, *Publisher*
Douglas Dentino, *Manager, New Product*

For more information, contact:
Greenhaven Press
27500 Drake Rd.
Farmington Hills, MI 48331-3535
Or you can visit our Internet site at gale.cengage.com

For product information and technology assistance, contact us at

Gale Customer Support, 1-800-877-4253
For permission to use material from this text or product, submit all requests online at www.cengage.com/permissions

Further permissions questions can be emailed to permissionrequest@cengage.com

Articles in Greenhaven Press anthologies are often edited for length to meet page requirements. In addition, original titles of these works are changed to clearly present the main thesis and to explicitly indicate the author's opinion. Every effort is made to ensure that Greenhaven Press accurately reflects the original intent of the authors. Every effort has been made to trace the owners of copyrighted material.

Cover image © Karl Dolenc/E+/Getty Images.

LIBRARY OF CONGRESS CATALOGING-IN-PUBLICATION DATA

Copyright Infringement / Carol Ullmann and Lynn M. Zott, Book Editors
    p. cm. -- (Opposing viewpoints)
    Summary: "Opposing Viewpoints is the leading source for libraries and classrooms in need of current-issue materials. The viewpoints are selected from a wide range of highly respected sources and publications"-- Provided by publisher. Includes bibliographical references and index.
    ISBN 978-0-7377-6650-9 (hardback) -- ISBN 978-0-7377-6651-6 (paperback)
    1. Copyright infringement. I. Ullmann, Carol, editor of compilation. II. Zott, Lynn M. (Lynn Marie), 1969- editor of compilation.
    K1485.C667 2013
    346.04'82--dc23
                                    2013037279

Contents

Why Consider Opposing Viewpoints?   11

Introduction   14

Chapter 1: What Constitutes Copyright Infringement?

Chapter Preface   19

1. Copyright Infringement Is Theft   22
   Jonathan Pink

2. Copyright Infringement Is Not Theft   28
   Ben Jones

3. Is Music Sampling Copyright Infringement?   33
   Maria Christine D. Aragones

4. If You've Ever Sold a Used iPod, You May   47
   Have Violated Copyright Law
   Marvin Ammori

5. Selling Used Digital Goods Is Protected   53
   by the First-Sale Doctrine
   Corynne McSherry

Periodical and Internet Sources Bibliography   58

Chapter 2: What Is the Economic Impact of Copyright Infringement?

Chapter Preface   60

1. Copyright Infringement Hurts the Economy   63
   Department for Professional Employees

2. The Negative Economic Effects of Copyright   73
   Infringement Are Overstated
   Julian Sanchez

3. Why Should We Stop Online Piracy?   83
   Matthew Yglesias

4. Copyright Infringement Litigation Creates   **88**
   Legal and Financial Burdens
   Eriq Gardner

5. Music Sales Are Hurt by Copyright Infringement   **100**
   Steven Seidenberg

Periodical and Internet Sources Bibliography   **111**

Chapter 3: Is Copyright Law Effective?

Chapter Preface   **113**

1. The Digital Millennium Copyright Act Protects   **115**
   Against Copyright Infringement
   Jeffrey D. Neuburger

2. The Digital Millennium Copyright Act   **126**
   Jeopardizes Fair Use
   Fred von Lohmann

3. The Copyright Alert System Will Prevent   **135**
   Copyright Infringement
   Recording Industry Association of America

4. The Copyright Alert System Violates   **141**
   Consumers' Rights and Will Not Stop
   Copyright Infringement
   Joey LeMay

5. Creative Commons Licensing   **147**
   Promotes Creative Works
   Glyn Moody

6. Innovate or Legislate   **152**
   Reihan Salam and Patrick Ruffini

Periodical and Internet Sources Bibliography   **167**

Chapter 4: How Does Technology Affect Copyright Infringement?

Chapter Preface   **169**

1. Peer-to-Peer Services Facilitate   171
   Copyright Infringement
   Kollin J. Zimmermann

2. Peer-to-Peer Services Can Be Legitimized   182
   Devindra Hardawar

3. Self-Published E-books Encourage   187
   Copyright Infringement
   Mike Essex

4. Copyright Infringement of E-books   195
   Is an Ethical Grey Area
   Martin Paul Eve

5. Copyright Policy Can Adapt to   202
   Changing Technology
   Laurence Kaye

6. Changing Technology Has Made Traditional   212
   Copyright Policy Obsolete
   Chad Perrin

Periodical and Internet Sources Bibliography   220

For Further Discussion   221

Organizations to Contact   224

Bibliography of Books   229

Index   233

Why Consider Opposing Viewpoints?

> *"The only way in which a human being can make some approach to knowing the whole of a subject is by hearing what can be said about it by persons of every variety of opinion and studying all modes in which it can be looked at by every character of mind. No wise man ever acquired his wisdom in any mode but this."*
>
> *John Stuart Mill*

In our media-intensive culture it is not difficult to find differing opinions. Thousands of newspapers and magazines and dozens of radio and television talk shows resound with differing points of view. The difficulty lies in deciding which opinion to agree with and which "experts" seem the most credible. The more inundated we become with differing opinions and claims, the more essential it is to hone critical reading and thinking skills to evaluate these ideas. Opposing Viewpoints books address this problem directly by presenting stimulating debates that can be used to enhance and teach these skills. The varied opinions contained in each book examine many different aspects of a single issue. While examining these conveniently edited opposing views, readers can develop critical thinking skills such as the ability to compare and contrast authors' credibility, facts, argumentation styles, use of persuasive techniques, and other stylistic tools. In short, the Opposing Viewpoints Series is an ideal way to attain the higher-level thinking and reading skills so essential in a culture of diverse and contradictory opinions.

In addition to providing a tool for critical thinking, Opposing Viewpoints books challenge readers to question their own strongly held opinions and assumptions. Most people form their opinions on the basis of upbringing, peer pressure, and personal, cultural, or professional bias. By reading carefully balanced opposing views, readers must directly confront new ideas as well as the opinions of those with whom they disagree. This is not to simplistically argue that everyone who reads opposing views will—or should—change his or her opinion. Instead, the series enhances readers' understanding of their own views by encouraging confrontation with opposing ideas. Careful examination of others' views can lead to the readers' understanding of the logical inconsistencies in their own opinions, perspective on why they hold an opinion, and the consideration of the possibility that their opinion requires further evaluation.

Evaluating Other Opinions

To ensure that this type of examination occurs, Opposing Viewpoints books present all types of opinions. Prominent spokespeople on different sides of each issue as well as well-known professionals from many disciplines challenge the reader. An additional goal of the series is to provide a forum for other, less known, or even unpopular viewpoints. The opinion of an ordinary person who has had to make the decision to cut off life support from a terminally ill relative, for example, may be just as valuable and provide just as much insight as a medical ethicist's professional opinion. The editors have two additional purposes in including these less known views. One, the editors encourage readers to respect others' opinions—even when not enhanced by professional credibility. It is only by reading or listening to and objectively evaluating others' ideas that one can determine whether they are worthy of consideration. Two, the inclusion of such viewpoints encourages the important critical thinking skill of objectively evaluating an author's credentials and bias. This evaluation will illuminate an author's reasons for taking a particular stance on an issue and will aid in readers' evaluation of the author's ideas.

It is our hope that these books will give readers a deeper understanding of the issues debated and an appreciation of the complexity of even seemingly simple issues when good and honest people disagree. This awareness is particularly important in a democratic society such as ours in which people enter into public debate to determine the common good. Those with whom one disagrees should not be regarded as enemies but rather as people whose views deserve careful examination and may shed light on one's own.

Thomas Jefferson once said that "difference of opinion leads to inquiry, and inquiry to truth." Jefferson, a broadly educated man, argued that "if a nation expects to be ignorant and free . . . it expects what never was and never will be." As individuals and as a nation, it is imperative that we consider the opinions of others and examine them with skill and discernment. The Opposing Viewpoints Series is intended to help readers achieve this goal.

David L. Bender and Bruno Leone,
Founders

Introduction

> *"The next great copyright act must be forward thinking but flexible. It should not attempt to answer the entire universe of possible questions, but, no matter what, it must serve the public interest. Thus, it must confirm and rationalize certain fundamental aspects of the law, including the ability of authors and their licensees to control and exploit their creative works, whether content is distributed on the street or streamed from the cloud. This control cannot be absolute, but it needs to be meaningful."*
>
> —*Maria Pallante,*
> *US Register of Copyrights*
> *"The Next Great Copyright Act,"*
> *Twenty-Sixth Horace S. Manges Lecture,*
> *March 4, 2013*

In 1976, the US Congress signed into law a deeply revised Copyright Act, giving creators exclusive rights to their works—whether published or unpublished—for their lifespan plus fifty years, thus granting their heirs for two generations the ability to collect income from their work. Corporate copyright was extended to seventy-five years from a work's creation. In the United States, copyright law protects the following original works: literary; musical (including accompanying words); dramatic (including accompanying music); pantomime and choreographic; pictorial, graphic, or sculptural; motion picture and audiovisual; sound recording; and architectural. Copyright does not protect an idea but the expression of an idea.

Personal computers and digital media became more prominent in American culture throughout the 1980s and 1990s, leading to the passage of the Digital Millennium Copyright Act (DMCA) in 1998. The DMCA sought to protect copyright material by criminalizing the production and distribution of devices that circumvent digital rights management (DRM), a general term for technology that controls access to copyright material. DRM and anticircumnavigation are controversial areas of law. Some argue that they are necessary to combat infringement, and others maintain that they impose unduly on legitimate consumers while remaining ineffective against infringers.

The Copyright Term Extension Act (CTEA) of 1998 was put into law on the same day as the DMCA and extended copyright protection for an additional 20 years; individual copyright was now the creator's lifespan plus 70 years and corporate copyright was 95 years from publication or 120 years from creation. This act was also known as the Sonny Bono Act in memory of the California congressman who supported it and who died months before its passage. As a former recording artist and actor, Bono had taken particular interest in copyright protection. The Walt Disney Company also lobbied for the CTEA, ostensibly to protect Mickey Mouse's earliest movies from passing into public domain. This gave the act its colloquial name of the Mickey Mouse Protection Act. "Steamboat Willie," Mickey Mouse's first film, was set to have its copyright expire in 2003, but is now under copyright protection until 2023. Despite efforts by many opposed to this extension, including law professor Dennis Karjala, publishers, and librarians, the CTEA passed and successfully weathered subsequent challenges to its constitutionality.

The Stop Online Piracy Act (SOPA) was a House bill introduced in October 2011 and was intended to give law enforcement greater ability to combat copyright infringement and the trafficking of counterfeit goods online. Sites alleged to be infringing could be shut down, have their advertising turned off, or have their payment mechanisms turned off while undergoing investigation. A similar bill, the Preventing Real Online Threats to Economic Creativity and Theft (PROTECT) of Intellectual Property Act (PIPA) was proposed in the Senate in May 2011. Opponents of SOPA/PIPA, including the Electronic Frontier Foundation (EFF), argued that these bills were too broad in their approach and threatened free speech, free enterprise, and innovation. Proponents of these bills, including the Hollywood film industry, argued that stronger controls were needed to battle online infringement, particularly from overseas infringers.

On January 18–19, 2012, thousands of websites—including Reddit, Wikipedia, Google, Mozilla, Craigslist, Boing Boing, Tumblr, Twitter, and Wordpress—participated in an oppositional blackout to demonstrate the potential state of the Internet under SOPA/PIPA. These websites were either completely disabled by their owners, leaving visitors with an error when they tried to load a page on the site, or their front page was covered by a written protest with normal content disabled or only available through a backdoor link. Additionally, thousands of people called or e-mailed their representatives and senators in Washington, with the heightened traffic crashing some politicians' websites. The blackout had its intended effect. Many representatives and senators switched their position on SOPA and PIPA, and these bills were effectively hung in their respective committees and never brought to a vote.

Despite endless rounds of litigation over copyrighted works and increasingly complex copyright case law, people continue to create. The viewpoints in *Opposing Viewpoints: Copyright Infringement* examine many of the issues surrounding how copyright infringement affects contemporary society. In the chapters that follow, "What Constitutes Copyright Infringement?," "What Is the Economic Impact of Copyright Infringement?," "Is Copyright Law Effective?," and "How Does Technology Affect Copyright Infringement?," writers debate the significance of infringement and innovation in the digital age.

OPPOSING
VIEWPOINTS®
SERIES

CHAPTER 1

What Constitutes Copyright Infringement?

Chapter Preface

Fair use is a doctrine in the Copyright Act that permits the use of copyright material without permission from or payment to the copyright holder under specific conditions. These conditions, set out in sections 107 through 118 of the act, include teaching, research, reporting, and criticism. While no detailed guidelines have ever been fixed by law as to what constitutes fair use, there are four general guidelines, set forth in section 107, to help individuals and courts decide whether a given use is fair or infringing:

1. the purpose and character of the use, including whether such use is of a commercial nature or is for nonprofit educational purposes;

2. the nature of the copyrighted work;

3. the amount and substantiality of the portion used in relation to the copyrighted work as a whole; and

4. the effect of the use upon the potential market for or value of the copyrighted work.

Fair use doctrine makes it possible for book reviewers or scholarly works to quote from copyrighted material, for teachers to share copyrighted content in the classroom, and for reporters to comment on and discuss works that are protected by copyright. In this way, a public dialogue can continue without fear of legal retribution. It can also help authors and artists achieve exposure; for example, book reviews in magazines and newspapers are one way people learn about new books they might like to purchase and read.

Copyright infringement is sometimes committed under the guise of fair use, but the grey areas of fair use stir up the most interest as people come to an understanding of what the spirit of the law does and does not protect. A landmark set of cases involving Internet giant Google began a national discussion of what fair use means in the digital age. In 2004, Google announced a project to scan and digitize the full text of 15 million books and magazines, working in conjunction with libraries around the United States. In 2005, Google was sued by the Association of American Publishers for infringing on copyrighted content; a parallel class-action suit was brought against Google by many authors for copyright infringement. By 2008, the universities participating in the Google book-scanning project had formed HathiTrust, a national digital library (*Hathi* is pronounced "hah-tee" and is the Hindi (Indian) word for "elephant"; elephants are renowned for their long memories). HathiTrust was in turn sued in 2011 by the Author's Guild for copyright infringement.

Google's defense that it was well within fair use to digitize this content came under close scrutiny because Google is a privately owned for-profit company. HathiTrust, on the other hand, was an online library backed by public educational institutions and was able to leverage its undeniably nonprofit status to a different conclusion. In fall 2012 Google settled out of court with five major American publishing houses and agreed to abide by the publishers' decisions as to whether any of their content would be digitized by Google. The parallel class-action lawsuit waged by authors against Google went unsettled during this time. HathiTrust, however, won its case in federal court and saw the suit by the Author's Guild dismissed. Justice Harold Baer Jr. of the U.S. District Court in New York found HathiTrust to be operating within the bounds of fair use, indicating permission to proceed with digitizing orphaned works—books that are out of print and whose copyright holders cannot be found or contacted for permission.

When Congress rewrote the Copyright Act in 1976, no one then knew of the digital revolution that was to come. While legal and judicial provisions have been made, confusion persists as to what exactly constitutes copyright infringement. For some it is a matter of syntax and definition, but for others infringement may be a matter of cultural divide and how ownership is perceived. The US government has yet to provide a standing definition of fair use or copyright infringement, and so these issues are the subject of much discussion, as evidenced by the viewpoints in this chapter, which debate whether copyright infringement equals theft, and whether music sampling and reselling digital goods qualify as copyright infringement.

| *"I find referring to copyright infringe-*
ment as 'theft' to be pretty precise."

Copyright Infringement Is Theft

Jonathan Pink

Jonathan Pink is a Los Angeles–based intellectual property attorney at Bryan Cave LLC. In the following viewpoint, Pink argues that denying that copyright infringement is theft is splitting hairs in an effort to be too precise. Such precision overlooks the intrinsic nature of infringement as a type of theft, according to the author. Pink illuminates civil and criminal infractions that result from theft of intellectual property, physical or not. He also points out that infringement is criminalized in the Copyright Act, and says that this indicates an intent by the government to prevent theft. Pink acknowledges that theft may not be the best term to describe copyright infringement, but he maintains that he hs not found a better one.

As you read, consider the following questions:

1. According to Pink, why do some people, like scholar David Llewelyn, say that copyright infringement is not theft?

2. How does Pink draw a connection between the dictionary definition of *theft* and defining copyright infringement as a type of theft?

3. In California, what civil law has a copyright infringer broken when he or she takes physical possession of a work, and crime has been committed, according to the author?

Is copyright infringement "theft"? What's your gut response?

Surprisingly, the current top dog at the Motion Picture Association of America (MPAA) has come out against describing infringement as "theft."

Umm, let me get this straight, taking something owned by someone else without their permission is not theft? So you walk into Target with your eye on a top-of-the-line camcorder, slip that puppy into your backpack, then walk out without paying for it, we call that what? I'm willing to bet that even the MPAA's Christopher Dodd would call that theft.

So what's different in the copyright context? I ask because Mr. Dodd is not a lone wolf in making this claim.

Splitting Hairs

The U.S. Supreme Court ruled in 1985 that infringement does not "easily" equate with theft. (See *Dowling v. United States* [1985], 473 U.S. 207, 217–218).

This is also the position taken by a noted IP [intellectual property] scholar, David Llewelyn (a professor at King's College London and Head of Intellectual Property at White & Case in its London office), who stated at the IP Law Asia Summit that infringing another's intellectual property should not be referred to as theft because infringement does not physically deprive the "author" of his/her physical work.

Now, most people would agree that copyright infringement is unlawful. (I'm not talking about instances of fair use, implied or express license, public domain, or protection under the DMCA [Digital Millennium Copyright Act], etc.). But at the same time, many folks have taken issue with calling infringement "theft" or even "piracy," believing that it's important to be precise in our language.

The Meaning of "Theft"

I find referring to copyright infringement as "theft" to be pretty precise. And I think the distinction about no physical possession of the work misses the point.

To parse [analyze] this, let's start with a standard definition for "theft."

According to thefreedictionary.com, theft (n.) means "1. The act or an instance of stealing; larceny." To steal (v.tr.), according to the same website, means "1. To take (the property of another) without right or permission." Property (n.) means "1. a. Something owned; a possession." Intellectual property (n.), just to close the loop, is defined as "an intangible asset, such as a copyright or patent."

So, applying these definitions: a copyright is a form of intellectual property; property is something owned; taking the property of another without permission is called stealing; and "stealing," by definition, is theft.

Theft Is Theft

Under a standard dictionary usage of the words at issue, copyright infringement equates to theft irrespective of whether the infringer obtained physical possession of the underlying work.

And this makes sense. Even if the infringer never obtains physical possession of any "tangible works of authorship" as defined by the Copyright Act (see 17 U.S.C. §§ 101, 102), the infringer still obtains "possession" of those intangible rights granted to the work's author under Section 106.

These include the valuable right to reproduce, distribute copies, and publicly perform the work, among others. And these are not ephemeral rights. They come with the right to receive something very tangible: money! One of the most important, underlying rights granted to any author is the right to profit from one's creation. When an infringer misappropriates a work, he/she also steals the royalties the author could have received but for the infringement.

Just to make this perfectly clear: you want a copy of the work, it will cost you. If you take it without paying, that's a physical deprivation to the author of the right to collect payment. How is this any different than taking the camcorder without paying for it? In both instances, the thief has taken for free, and without permission, something of monetary value that the owner of that item sought to exchange for a price.

Physical Possession Does Not Matter

The fact that the infringer does not take physical possession of the copyrighted work itself should not matter when defining infringement as "theft." Indeed, taking physical possession of the work is separately actionable (civilly) under California law as conversion—or criminally as a theft.

A claim for conversion requires that a plaintiff establish: (1) the plaintiff's ownership or right to possession of certain property; (2) the defendant's conversion of the property by a wrongful act or disposition of property rights; and (3) damages. . . .

And interestingly, a claim for conversion is generally distinct enough from a claim for copyright infringement that it is immune from preemption under Section 303 of the Copyright Act. The reason it is immune is because it is a different type of theft—one that involves tangible property, not an intangible such as the right to exploit the work itself.

Also of note, the immunity from preemption for conversion disappears where the plaintiff seeks damages for reproduction of the property—not return of tangible property itself. . . . In those instances, conversion and infringement merge (the rights address in the conversion claim are deemed the same as those protected by the Copyright Act), and thus the conversion claim would be preempted. . . .

So there's no reason to preclude use of the word "theft" vis-à-vis infringement absent a physical taking, especially given we already have a civil term for that sort of conduct: conversion; and that sort of physical theft can exist side-by-side with the more ephemeral theft called infringement.

The Copyright Act Itself Agrees

Finally, the Copyright Act itself lends some support to the position that infringement amounts to a "theft," although it does so somewhat obliquely: All of us learn from an early age that stealing can land you in the pokey. Law enforcement is very concerned with the prevention of theft and punishing thieves. Agreed? So I find it interesting that the Copyright Act likewise has a criminal infringement component.

17 U.S.C. Section 506 states, in relevant part, that "Any person who willfully infringes a copyright shall be punished [criminally] as provided under section 2319 of title 18, if the infringement was committed—(A) for purposes of commercial advantage or private financial gain; (B) by the reproduction or distribution, including by electronic means, during any 180-day period, of 1 or more copies or phonorecords of 1 or more copyrighted works, which have a total retail value of more than $1,000; or (C) by the distribution of a work being prepared for commercial distribution, by making it available on a computer network accessible to members of the public, if such person knew or should have known that the work was intended for commercial distribution."

While I understand that infringement does not typically amount to "theft" in the sense that the copyright owner is deprived of his/her physical work, physical deprivation is not required to meet the dictionary definition of "theft." The fact that the copyright owner is deprived of his/her ability to receive compensation for the work, deprived of his/her right to control the distribution of the work, deprived of his/her ability to control the republishing and public performance of the work are all instances in which there has been a "stealing" of property rights. I see nothing wrong with calling that what it is: a theft.

Is "theft" the best word to convey what occurs through the act of infringement? It isn't bad, and I've yet to hear better.

> *"If copyright infringement was theft, then it would be treated as theft, dealt with as theft, and [the term] 'copyright infringement' wouldn't exist at all."*

Copyright Infringement Is Not Theft

Ben Jones

Ben Jones is a writer and engineer living in the Great Britain. He is a regular contributor to TorrentFreak, *a website dedicated to the file-sharing protocol BitTorrent. In the following viewpoint, Jones illustrates the procedural differences between trying a person for infringement versus trying a person for theft. First he outlines how a civil infringement trial works, using the Recording Industry Association of America case against Jammie Thomas-Rasset as an example. Jones underlines how civil infringement cases take longer, cost more, and tend to benefit the industry in damages and outcome. A hypothetical criminal theft trial based on the same case, by contrast, would be shorter and, if found in the prosecutor's favor, would cost the defendant significantly less, according to Jones. He concludes that careless comments equating infringement with theft only serve to stir up emotion and have no real legal basis.*

As you read, consider the following questions:

1. According to the author, in the Thomas-Rassett infringement case, what were the per-track damages determined by three different juries?

2. If the Thomas-Rassett case were dealt with as theft, what would the total value of the theft be, according to Jones?

3. For what reasons does a civil suit serve the industry better than a criminal trial, in the author's opinion?

A common recurring theme in the comments here on *TorrentFreak* is that P2P [peer-to-peer] file-sharing is 'stealing'. While such sentiments are often expressed by the industry lobby groups, it's completely at odds with the law. It could also be the very *last* thing those bodies want.

We get a lot of comments on articles from people saying things like "Yeah, it's stealing. Just embrace it already" or "Good excuse to steal right?"

There are editorials in mainstream newspapers that say "Such theft costs the copyright- or trademark-holders billions of dollars each year."

Even Vice President [Joe] Biden said last year [2010] that "Piracy is theft, clean and simple, it's smash and grab." But you'd think a longtime lawyer and member of the Senate Judiciary [Committee] would know to read the law.

The fact is that if copyright infringement was theft, then it would be treated as theft, dealt with as theft, and 'copyright infringement' wouldn't exist at all. Nevertheless, the claims are often made. We've dealt with this topic before three years ago, focusing on UK law. So let's take an example of a US case and see what would happen if it were tried as theft, instead of copyright infringement. The most obvious case is that of the RIAA [Recording Industry Association of America] against Jammie Thomas[-Rasset].

Illegal Downloading Should Not Be Labeled "Theft"

Illegal downloading is, of course, a real problem. . . . But framing illegal downloading as a form of stealing doesn't, and probably never will, work. We would do better to consider a range of legal concepts that fit the problem more appropriately: concepts like unauthorized use, trespass, conversion and misappropriation.

Stuart P. Green, New York Times, *March 29, 2012.*

A Civil Trial Benefits the Industry

We all know the process. A John Doe [a fictitious name used for an anonymous or unknown person] suit is filed (over 200,000 of them in the US so far), usually amalgamated into a group for easy processing (although it is legally questionable). This then goes to discovery, where the identity [of John Doe] is uncovered. At this point the suit is dropped and a direct appeal for 'settlement' is made. If no settlement is reached then the civil lawsuit process can be started.

In the Thomas case the civil lawsuit was filed April 2006, and has now gone on for several years; the latest activity [having taken place] just this last week [August 27, 2011]. Civil law provides for both actual damages *and* statutory damages from $200 to $30,000 for non-willful infringement and $750–$150,000 for willful infringement—per infringement. In three trials, juries have set the per-track damages figure for Thomas-Rasset at $9,250, $80,000 and $62,500 while the courts have twice reduced it to $2,250 per track, which the RIAA is appealing, *again.*

The case has now been ongoing for over 5 years, not counting the original John Doe complaint, and it has occupied hundreds if not thousands of man-hours defending it. These hours cost money, and in a civil case that means finding a lawyer willing to take it on pro bono [for free].

At first, Thomas-Rasset retained Brian Toder as her attorney, and later switched to Kiwi Camara. The much shorter *Capitol v. Foster* case had attorney costs of over $68,000 awarded after the RIAA dropped the case, while *Atlantic v Anderson* (dropped by the RIAA after 3 years) ended up with over $100,000 in costs awarded by the court.

As with all such cases the verdict is based on "balance of the probabilities" or 'preponderance of the evidence'. Quite a contrast to a criminal case.

A Criminal Trial Benefits the Infringer

Were copyright infringement "stealing," this would be the process Thomas-Rasset would undergo.

An investigation would be made by the police (rather than a private company hired by the complainant). As infringement is 'theft' she would be dealt with under Minnesota state law, specifically Minnesota Statute §609.52. She would be arrested, charged, and taken to court. If she could not afford a lawyer, one would be provided for her. Odds are, she would be dealt with in a matter of weeks, if not days.

The theft statute values goods at the cost to buy, so the 24 tracks would each be valued at $0.99—the cost on iTunes—for a total of $23.76. If we take the worst case scenario though, and assume a whole CD per track at $20 per CD, that still brings the total value of the theft to $480. As the value is below $500, the maximum penalty available is stipulated as follows:

> In all other cases where the value of the property or services stolen is $500 or less, to imprisonment for not more than 90 days or to payment of a fine of not more than $1,000, or both.

The trial would be judged, not on 'balance of the probabilities' as with a civil trial, but 'beyond reasonable doubt.' Based on the evidence submitted in the trials so far, such a case would fail, as Ms. Thomas-Rasset has never been proved to be personally responsible, only her connection and computer.

The Emotional Impact of Using *Theft*

Of course, if it were just a choice of a civil suit or a criminal theft trial, then it's clear why a civil trial is preferred, even if it is a money sink. Yet, there's one last obstacle: The Supreme Court of the US.

In 1985, the Court ruled in *Dowling v. United States* that copyright infringement is not theft, even when dealing with physical objects, such as vinyl records.

While industry bodies might still want to claim it's still theft there is one simple fact that's clear. In treating it as theft the benefit would be to the alleged infringer. A higher evidence standard, an independent investigation, legal counsel provided free for the alleged infringer, and vastly smaller penalties.

The infringement = theft argument has only one thing going for it, and that's its emotional impact. In reality, it's the very *last* thing they want, which is why new laws, like Protect IP and others have been pushed for many years. And again, we reiterate that we've dealt with the US here, laws for other countries are different, as we've seen twice in the past week in Sweden, yet it's still copyright infringement there, not theft.

> *"Any sample of a copyrighted work, regardless of its quantitative significance, may result in copyright infringement."*

Is Music Sampling Copyright Infringement?

Maria Christine D. Aragones

Maria Christine D. Aragones writes for IP Views, *an online periodical hosted by Bengzon Negre Untalan, an intellectual property law office in Manila, Philippines. In the following viewpoint, Aragones dispels the myth of the three-second rule—which posits that using three seconds or less of a musical work is considered fair use and not infringement—and cites court cases that have shaped how music sampling infringement is treated in the United States. Substantial similarity is the basis for many rulings in music sampling infringement cases and is appropriate when there is no literal copying, argues Aragones. More significant with sampling in the digital age is the fragmented literal similarity standard in which courts determine whether the sampled music is recognizable in the new work as coming from the original work. Aragones contends that the best defense mounted to date has been* de minimis, *which holds that the sample is too small to be considered substantially similar and therefore an in-*

Maria Christine D. Aragones, "Is Music Sampling Copyright Infringement?," *IP Views*, May 19, 2011. Copyright © 2011 by Bengzon Negre Untalan. All rights reserved. Reproduced by permission.

fringement. Nonetheless, Aragones concludes, the US Court of Appeals ruled in 2005 that musicians "Get a license or do not sample" as a bright line test to prevent costly copyright infringement cases.

As you read, consider the following questions:

1. According to Aragones, how long have some segments of sampled music that have been argued to infringe on copyright been?

2. What is *de minimis* use and how is it used as a defense against copyright infringement, according to the author?

3. What is the bright line test of music sampling, according to Aragones, and which case did it emerge from?

In an age characterized by rapid technological innovation, the protection of intellectual property, particularly copyrights, has become a major concern not just for big industry players but for individuals (i.e. artists, musicians, performers, etc.) as well. This article will hopefully shed light upon an issue that has preoccupied the music industry: "music sampling," or "digital sampling."

What Is "Sampling"

Music sampling simply means incorporating pre-existing recordings into a new recording, whether part or all of a tune (a melody) and/or the lyrics.[1] More often than not, sampling involves the incorporation of a short segment of a musical recording into a new musical recording.[2] In more technical terms, this involves:

"The conversion of analog sound waves into a digital code. The digital code that describes the sampled music . . . can then be revised, manipulated or combined with other digitalized or recorded sounds using a machine with digital data processing capabilities such as a . . . computerized synthesizer."[3]

Sampling Emerged from Jamaican Toasting

Much of hip-hop, R'n'B and rap music is created using samples—snippets from pre-recorded music: a tune, parts or lines from the lyrics of a song, among others. Take Rihanna's hit single "Please Don't Stop the Music", for instance. The song contains a line, "Ma Ma Se, Ma Ma Sa, Ma Ma Coo Sa," which was sampled from the late Michael Jackson's 1983 song "Wanna Be Startin' Something", also reportedly sourced from an even earlier song by Manu Dibango[4] entitled "Soul Makossa" of 1972.[5]

The practice of sampling music is said to have originated from Jamaica in the 1960s when it was done through portable sound systems. In its earliest forms, Jamaican disc jockeys (the "DJ") would play records with a recognizable drum and bass line and another person (the "MC") would utter words and lyrics over the rhythm and melodies. This practice, known as "toasting," predated the birth of hip hop in the 1970's. When hip hop started, DJs would sample music using analog technology, particularly analog turntables and mixers.[6] The practice became more prevalent in the 1980s with the use of digital synthesizers equipped with Musical Instrument Digital Interface ("MIDI"). The use of digital synthesizers enabled artists not just to mix sounds from a pre-existing recording but to isolate unique sounds from a musical recording.[7] Since then, music sampling through digital recording pioneered much of the music as we know it today.

Battling Copyright Issues

As vigilance over copyrights intensified in the music industry, copyright-owners have sued artists, recording companies, and producers who have used samples or recognizable elements of their copyrighted work without authorization.

The U.S. Copyright Act of 1976 provides that musical works[8] and sound recordings[9] which are original and fixed in any tangible medium of expression, now known or later developed from which they can be perceived, reproduced, or otherwise communicated, either directly or with the aid of a machine or device[10] shall be protected. This means that in any given sample, there are two subsisting copyrights: 1) over the composition itself (i.e., the "compositional copyright") and 2) over the sound recording (i.e., the "sound recording copyright"). The compositional copyright is usually owned by the composer of the song. Copyright to the sound recording, on the other hand, is usually owned by the recording company or the producer of the sound recording.

The U.S. statute affords the copyright-owner the exclusive rights to do and to authorize any of the following:

1. to reproduce the copyrighted work in copies or phonorecords;

2. to prepare derivative works based upon the copyrighted work;

3. to distribute copies or phonorecords of the copyrighted work to the public by sale or other transfer of ownership, or by rental, lease, or lending;

4. in the case of literary, musical, dramatic, and choreographic works, pantomimes, and motion pictures and other audiovisual works, to perform the copyrighted work publicly;

5. in the case of literary, musical, dramatic, and choreographic works, pantomimes, and pictorial, graphic, or sculptural works, including the individual images of a motion picture or other audiovisual work, to display the copyrighted work publicly; and

6. in the case of sound recordings, to perform the copyrighted work publicly by means of a digital audio transmission.[11]

However, a person owning a copyright to the sound recording only has the right to duplicate a sound recording in the form of phonorecords that directly or indirectly recapture the actual sounds fixed in the recording.[12]

"The Three-Second Rule"

To begin with, sources within and outside the music industry have said that in practice, a sample that does not exceed 3 seconds is either not actionable or is not actively prosecuted. This remains an unwritten rule, and is neither supported by law nor jurisprudence.[13] The sampling of even the smallest segments of a musical recording, such as a tune, a three-note sequence, a guitar riff or part of the lyrics of a song, has long been the subject of lawsuits.[14] Although most sampling cases often end up being settled out of court,[15] jurisprudence is replete with discussions on the matter.

The Substantial Familiarity Test

In most cases,[16] a court assesses whether the work containing the sample is substantially similar to the original work from which the sample was taken to determine whether the sampling is actionable. The test of similarity is a test of first impression,[17] which considers the separate works in their entirety.[18] Similarity between the two works occurs when the overall structure or theme of the musical recording or composition is used but there has been no literal copying ("comprehensive non-literal copying") or when a portion of the copyrighted work (usually a small portion as in most digital sampling cases) has been copied literally ("fragmented literal similarity").[19]

The determination of whether substantial similarity exists specifically rests on a quantitative and qualitative analysis of the sample in relation to the entire copyrighted work. Quantitative analysis is concerned with how much of the plaintiff's work is copied while qualitative analysis is concerned with the significance of the portion taken to the whole work.[20] This is especially true where the copyright alleged to have been infringed is the compositional copyright.[21]

An Alternative Test: Fragmental Familiarity Standard

In 2009, the United States Court of Appeals, Sixth Circuit, had occasion to employ a different standard in determining substantial similarity in the unique case of *Bridgeport v. UMG Recording Inc.*[22] The case involved George Clinton's "Atomic Dog" (considered by many to be a quintessential funk anthem). A hip hop band used the "Bow Wow refrain" ("Bow wow wow yippie yo, yippie yea") as well as the repetition of the word "dog" in a low tone voice at regular intervals.[23] The case is unique because "Atomic Dog" was created spontaneously in the recording studio and there was no written score or lyrics sheet created until after the sound recording was released.

The court affirmed the use of the fragmented literal similarity standard in finding that there was substantial similarity between the two works and, consequently, infringement. The test was applied since there was a literal copying of a portion of the original work.[24] In cases where fragmented literal similarity occurs, the court evaluates whether the portion that has been copied literally is recognizable by an ordinary reasonable person as having been appropriated from the original work. In the present case, the court held that the elements copied, although relatively small portions, were not only original but, at the same time, the most distinctive and recognizable elements of the original composition.

Applying the fragmented literal similarity test would suggest that any sample of a copyrighted work, regardless of its quantitative significance, may result in copyright infringement when it constitutes a substantial part of the sampled original work.

De Minimis Use

Corollary to the substantial similarity test is the defense that the copying only amounts to a de minimis taking, or is so trivial as to be unactionable. *Newton v. Diamond*[25] held that:

"To establish that the infringement of a copyright is de minimis, and therefore not actionable, the alleged infringer must demonstrate that the copying of the protected material is so trivial "as to fall below the quantitative threshold of substantial similarity. . . . No "substantial similarity [will] be found if only a small, common phrase appears in both the accused and complaining songs . . . unless the reappearing phrase is especially unique or qualitatively important." . . . A taking is de minimis if the average audience would not recognize the misappropriation."

De minimis, when used as a defense in a sampling lawsuit, would mean that the amount that has been sampled is believed to have been minimal and that the portion(s) copied are not important or significant to the copyrighted work such that it would barely be recognized by an average listener.

In *Newton*[26], a 3-note sequence from James W. Newton's musical composition entitled "Choir" was sampled by the famous rap group Beastie Boys in their work "Pass the Mic." The sample, which appeared only once at the beginning and lasted for only 6 seconds of the 4 and a half-minute-long original musical composition, was not significant enough to constitute infringement.[27] The court found that it was neither quantitatively nor qualitatively substantial to be actionable. The use of the sample, therefore, was de minimis.

Another case, *Jean et al. v. Bug Music*,[28] affirmed the de minimis defense. Bug Music (the defendants) initially sued the authors (plaintiffs) of a song popularized by Whitney Houston and claimed that it infringed a song they wrote several years ago. Specifically, the infringing song contained the lyrical and musical excerpt: "Clap your hand, y'all, 't's' all right" which closely resembled that contained in Bug Music's work

"Hand Clapping Song". The court granted plaintiff's petition for a summary judgment and ruled that the phrase "clap your hands now, people clap now" is a common phrase that often appeared in church and secular music, hence, it was neither original nor copyrightable. The court also held that listeners would also not have recognized that the sampled portions came from the defendant's work. The songs sounded different and engendered different responses from the audience.[29] Hence, the case was dismissed on the ground that the use is de minimis.[30]

Boone v. Jackson,[31] although it did not explicitly use the words 'de minimis', arrived at a similar conclusion. Here, the court held that use of the phrase "holla back" in an eight-note syncopated rhythm in the hook of a rap song did not amount to an infringement of an earlier work. Not only was the phrase common and hence unprotectable by copyright, but even as it were, the works are not substantially similar to a lay observer (The court found that aside from the repeated use of the phrase, the works overall qualities were significantly dissimilar).[32]

From these rulings, it can be inferred that the use of ordinary, common phrases and common components of various melodies may be classified as de minimis. They do not merit any copyright protection probably because such phrases are not original and are not an integral part of the song.

The split in the jurisprudence on digital sampling was occasioned by the *Bridgeport Music, Inc. v. Dimension Films*[33] ruling in 2005, which involved an infringement claim of a copyright to a sound recording. The United States Court of Appeals for the 6th circuit overturned the district court's ruling, which held that the defendant's sampling of a guitar riff from the musical recording did not "rise to the level of copyright infringement under either of two standards: the de minimis analysis or the fragmented literal similarity test." In its decision, the appellate court distinguished between an action for infringement of a copyright to a musical composition and an action for infringement of a copyright to a sound recording. It held that the standards used to determine infringement of a copyright to a musical composition (i.e. the de minimis analysis or the fragmented literal similarity test) was inapplicable to an infringement case involving a copyright to a sound recording.

In this case, the court, ignoring previous case law on music sampling, decided that in instances affecting the copyrights to a sound recording, the only issue is whether the actual sound recording has been used without authorization. Hence, the test is more direct, so to speak, such that every instance of unauthorized digital sampling, even when the sampled portion is hardly recognizable,[34] would be a violation of the copyright to the sound recording. The U.S. Court of Appeals for the 6th circuit in *Bridgeport* held that digital sampling is "never accidental" and that "the appropriation is a physical taking rather than an intellectual one."[36] Therefore, the question of whether or not the sample is recognizable by an average lay person (i.e. applying the substantial similarity test) will not factor in the assessment.

No actual case applying the doctrine enunciated in *Bridgeport Music, Inc. v. Dimension Films* has been reported to date. The appellate court in the case veered away from previous rulings on cases involving music sampling when it opted not to apply the substantial similarity test. Based on its own interpretation of the U.S. copyright law,[37] the court created a "bright line test" previously unheard of. "Get a license or do not sample."

However, a case predating *Bridgeport* and its bright line test came to a somewhat similar conclusion. *Grand Upright Music, Ltd. V. Warner Bros. Records, Inc.*[38] showed that proof of copyright ownership and unauthorized sampling is enough to constitute infringement. The court therein held that ". . . the most persuasive evidence that the copyrights are valid and owned by the plaintiff comes from the actions and admissions of the defendants". Documentary evidence also showed that the defendants tried to obtain the permission of the owner. However, their album, which contained the infringing work, was released pending the application for the license. Hence, the court ruled that the infringement was willful. For this, many have criticized the *Grand Upright* ruling as a bad precedent.[39]

Follow the Bright Line?

Although the general "consensus" among recording artists and companies was to choose "obscure enough" samples such as would be unrecognizable,[40] most artists now simply choose to follow the "bright line test" to avoid being entangled in copyright lawsuits. For this purpose, they would try to obtain clearances for samples from copyright-owners: 1) the copyright owner of the song and 2) the copyright owner of the master recording.[41] Although obtaining sample clearances may be a tedious task, it is less taxing and less expensive in the long run. Organizations in the U.S. such as the Broadcast Music Incorporated (BMI) or the American Society of Composers, Authors, and Publishers (ASCAP) help a great deal in obtaining sampling clearances from song publishers. The publishers themselves or the record company that released the album(s) containing the work sought to be sampled can help in tracking down the copyright-owner of the master recording. Otherwise, online records, databases and directories may prove useful.

Notes

1. Ben Challis, The Song Remains the Same: A Review of the Legalities of Music Sampling, available at http://www.wipo.int/wipo_magazine/en/2009/article_0006.html (last accessed May 10, 2011).
2. Newton v. Diamond, 204 F. Supp. 2d 1244 (2004).

3. Peter Cuomo. Legal Update: Claiming Infringement Over Three Notes Is Not Preaching to the "Choir": Newton v. Diamond and A Potential New Standard in Copyright Law (citing Jarvis v. A&M Records, 827 F. Supp. 282, 286 (D.N.J. 1993)), available at http://www.bu.edu/law/central/jd/organizations/journals/scitech/volume101/cuomo.pdf (last accessed May 12, 2011).

4. Manu Dibango is a popular Cameroonian saxophonist of the 1970s.

5. Tom Breihan, Manu Dibango Sues Rihanna, Michael Jackson available at http://pitchfork.com/news/34538-manu-dibango-sues-rihanna-michael-jackson/ (last accessed on May 12, 2011).

6. John Lindenbaum, Music Sampling and Copyright Law (1999) (Unpublished thesis, Princeton University) (available at http://www.princeton.edu/~artspol/studentpap/undergrad%20thesis1%20JLind.pdf).

7. Id.

8. 17 U.S.C. Sec 102(a).

9. Id.

10. Id.

11. 17 U.S.C. Sec 106 (1).

12. Robert A. Gorman, Copyright Law Second Edition available at http://www.scribd.com/doc/8763709/copyright-law-second-edition (last accessed on May 11, 2011).

13. supra note 1.

14. Newton v. Diamond, 204 F. Supp. 2d 1244 (2004).

15. It has been reported that the late Michael Jackson settled his case with Manu Dibango (Tom Breihan, Manu Dibango Sues Rihanna, Michael Jackson available at http://pitchfork.com/news/34538-manu-dibango-sues-rihanna-michael-jackson/ (last accessed on May 12, 2011)).

16. Such test was ignored in the case of Grand Upright Music, Ltd. vs. Warner Brothers Records, Inc. (780 F. Supp. 182) and Bridgeport Music, Inc. v. Diamond Films (410 F.3d 792 (6th Cir. 2005).

17. The court considers whether the average lay observer would recognize the appropriation.
18. In the case of Jean, et al. vs. Bug Music (No. 00 Civ 4022(DC), 2002 WL 287786 (S.D.N.Y. Feb. 27, 2002)), the songs were evaluated based on the sounds and the mood that each song conveyed.
19. Stephen R. Wilson, Music Sampling Lawsuits: Does looping music samples defeat the de minimis defense?, The Journal of High Technology Law, available at http://www.thefreelibrary.com/_/print/PrintArticle.aspx?=id17259 9157 (last accessed on May 16, 2011).
20. Id.
21. The case of Newton vs. Diamond used this type of analysis to come to the conclusion that the Beastie Boys' song which contained a three-note sample from James Newton's composition and the original composition were not substantially similar (Quantitatively: the portion sampled lasted approximately two seconds and comprised roughly two percent of Newton's composition; Qualitatively: the portion was not more important to Newton's composition that any other portion).
22. No. 07-5596 (C.A. 6, Nov. 4, 2009).
23. Bridgeport Music, Inc. v. UMG Recording, Inc., No. 07-5596 (2009).
24. supra note 18
25. 204. F. Supp. 2d 1244 (2004).
26. Id.
27. The court held that the excerpt was "merely a common, trite, and generic three note sequence, which lacks any distinct, melodic, harmonious, rhythmic or structural elements . . . a common building block tool that has been used over and over again by major composers in the 20th century."
28. (No. 00 Civ 4022(DC), 2002 WL 287786 (S.D.N.Y. Feb. 27, 2002).

29. The Hand Clapping Song was a funk song characterized by strong percussion and guitar sounds and invited the listener to clap their hands in time with the beat. On the other hand, the allegedly infringing song "My Love is Your Love" sounded more mellow "with a smooth bass line accompanied by soft percussion".

30. UCLA School of law available at http://cip.law.ucla.edu/cases/2000-2009/Pages/jeanbugmusic.aspx (last accessed on May 17, 2011).

31. No. 03 Civ. 8661 (S.D.N.Y. July 1, 2005).

32. David J. Moser, Case Study: Boone v. Jackson (Fabolous)–Holla Back Copyright (citing Boone v. Jackson No. 03 Civ 8661 (S.D.N.Y. July 1, 2005), available at http://www.copyrightguru.com/belmont_classes/IntellectualProperties/Cases/BoonevJackson.pdf (last accessed May 16, 2011).

33. 410 F.3d 792 (6th Cir. 2005).

34. The segment taken was altered: the pitch was lowered and the piece was looped so that it would last for approximately 7 seconds in the subsequent recording.

35. Interpreting the law, it would appear that the copyright-owner of a sound recording has the exclusive right to "re-record" his sound recording.

36. Nicole Stafford, Intellectual Property Law–Copyright infringement–Any Digital Sample of Music Taken From a Sound Recording is Prohibited Under the Federal Copyright Statute, 17 U.S.C §114. Bridgeport Music, Inc. v. Dimension Films, 410 F.3d 37 792 (6th Cir. 2005), available at http://www.law.udmercy.edu/lawreview/recentissues/v84/issue1/84_udm_law_review_rev35.pdf (last accessed on May 12, 2011).

37. The Copyright Act of 1976, 17 U.S.C. Sec. 114.

38. 780 F. Supp. 182 (S.D.N.Y. 1991).

39. Wikipedia, the free encyclopedia, available at http://en.wikipedia.org/wiki/Grand_Upright_Music,_Ltd._v._Warner_Bros._Records_Inc. (last accessed May 17,2011).

40. Supra note 18 (citing Markkus Rovito, Bomb Tracks: A Hip-Hop How To, REMIX, June 1, 2001, at 64-66).

41. Obtaining Persmission before Sampling Music, available at http://smallbusiness.findlaw.com/copyright/copyright-realworld/music-sampling-permission.html (last accessed May 12, 2011).

*"A copyright logo ... empowers manu-
facturers to sue people for copyright infringement for unlawful sales."*

If You've Ever Sold a Used iPod, You May Have Violated Copyright Law

Marvin Ammori

*Marvin Ammori is a First Amendment lawyer and a legal fellow
at the New America Foundation's Open Technology Initiative. In
the following viewpoint, Ammori presents common examples of
digital goods that people regularly sell used, which, he explains,
violates copyright because these goods were manufactured abroad
and are therefore not protected by the first-sale doctrine. The author outlines three court cases that have dealt with the issues of
first-sale doctrine and foreign imports, with each case coming to
a different conclusion and leading to further confusion over what
is enforceable. Ammori urges courts to come to a clear conclusion
and not leave this matter up to Congress. The Supreme Court
later ruled that products made overseas are subject to the first-
sale doctrine.*

As you read, consider the following questions:

1. According to Ammori, what is the first-sale doctrine and why is it currently being contested?

2. What New York federal court case found that first-sale doctrine does not apply to copyrighted products manufactured abroad, according to the author?

3. How did watchmaker Omega seek to protect its expensive watches from being sold at lower prices in the United States, according to Ammori?

The Supreme Court will soon hear a case that will affect whether you can sell your iPad—or almost anything else—without needing to get permission from a dozen "copyright holders." Here are some things you might have recently done that will be rendered illegal if the Supreme Court upholds the lower court decision:

1. Sold your first-generation iPad on Craigslist to a willing buyer, even if you bought the iPad lawfully at the Apple Store.

2. Sold your dad's used Omega watch on eBay to buy him a fancier (used or new) Rolex at a local jewelry store.

3. Sold an "import CD" of your favorite band that was only released abroad but legally purchased there. Ditto for a copy of a French or Spanish novel not released in the U.S.

4. Sold your house to a willing buyer, so long as you sell your house along with the fixtures manufactured in China, a chandelier made in Thailand or Paris, support beams produced in Canada that carry the imprint of a copyrighted logo, or a bricks or a marble countertop made in Italy with any copyrighted features or insignia.

Here is what's going on.

Digital Music Is Not Owned by the Buyer

"Purchasing" a song on, say, iTunes does not mean you've bought the song itself. Instead, you've paid for the right to play that song in your personal life . . . It is—believe it or not—against the law to burn a copy of a song you "purchased" onto a CD, or to give a licensed MP3 file to a friend.

Andrew Couts, Digital Trends,
November 1, 2012. www.digitaltrends.com.

The Supreme Court case concerns something called the "first-sale doctrine" in copyright law. Simply put, the doctrine means that you can buy and sell the stuff you purchase. Even if someone has copyright over some piece of your stuff, you can sell it without permission from the copyright holder because the copyright holder can only control the "first-sale." The Supreme Court has recognized this doctrine since 1908.

To use a classic example, imagine you buy a novel by Sabina Murray. Sabina owns the copyright to the book, so you can't make a copy of the book. But you bought a copy of the book, and can sell the copy to anyone who'll pay you for it. You can sell it to a neighbor, to a fellow student, or to someone else on Craigslist or on eBay.

But the first-sale rule doesn't just make it possible to sell your books and other creative works like CDs, paintings, or DVDs. Almost every product made now has a copyright logo on it. That logo, alone, empowers manufacturers to sue people for copyright infringement for unlawful sales.

The first-sale doctrine is one thing that makes it lawful to sell almost any good. The companies that have gone to court and sued over selling their "copyrights" include a watchmaker and shampoo producer. They have gone to court arguing that one part of the Copyright Act—which gives them a right against unauthorized imports—invalidates the first-sale doctrine.

In 1998, the Supreme Court ruled that the first-sale doctrine applies to any product manufactured in the United States, sold in the U.S., even if the first sale by the copyright holder was abroad and the item was imported back into the U.S. This decision was unanimous and rejected the interpretation preferred by the U.S. government's lawyer—and the biggest copyright holders.

The legal confusion today concerns only products made abroad.

Continuing a long string of similar cases, the Supreme Court will review a New York federal court decision that decided, in short, that the first-sale doctrine does not apply to any copyrighted product manufactured abroad. That case concerns textbooks.

John Wiley & Sons, a textbook publisher, sells expensive versions of the textbooks here and less expensive versions abroad. Supap Kirtsaeng, a foreign graduate student at University of Southern California, decided to help pay for his schooling by having relatives buy him copies of the foreign versions abroad, send them to him, whereupon he'd sell those books on eBay to willing students. He'd make money, the students would save money, but Wiley might have fewer sales of its pricey American versions. The case is styled *Kirtsaeng v. John Wiley & Sons.*

Both the District and Second Circuit courts held that any product manufactured abroad is not subject to the first-sale doctrine. For instance, that iPad you sold. You noticed this statement: "Designed by Apple in California. Assembled in China." Same for the iPods you've owned, the iPhones, and the MacBooks. Because those products were manufactured abroad, according to the Second Circuit, the first-sale doctrine doesn't apply to them. You need the permission of every copyright holder to sell the iPad.

That means, you need to ask Apple for permission, and probably Google, whose Maps software comes bundled with the iPad, and includes Google copyrights. Under this rule, when you sell some of your stuff on eBay or Craigslist (a couch, some books, electronics, posters, an old television, a toaster), you have to look up whether it has a copyrighted logo anywhere and find out whether the product was manufactured in the U.S. or abroad.

The lower court decision did acknowledge "the force of the concern" that the rule would lead to more companies moving manufacturing abroad, and noted that the law was particularly unclear. But it decided that, if its interpretation of the law should lead to these bizarre conclusions, Congress could sort it out later, which is little comfort considering Congress has a lot to do, and relies on courts not interpreting laws in ways that lead to completely absurd results.

The Omega example comes from a real decision in a California case from the Ninth Circuit. Omega, the Swiss maker of fancy watches, sued Costco, a major retailer, for selling real Omega watches that had a copyrighted logo underneath the watch face. A distributor bought the Omega watches abroad and eventually Costco bought them to sell at a price still lower than what you would pay at an Omega store here in the U.S.

To ensure that Americans pay more for Omegas than people in other parts of the world, Omega sued Costco. That court decided that anything manufactured abroad and authorized only to be sold abroad, not in the U.S., is not subject to the first-sale doctrine in the U.S. The Supreme Court decided to review the *Costco v. Omega* case back in 2010, but deadlocked at four votes against, four in favor, with Justice Elena Kagan having to sit out the decision because of previous government work on the case.

There is actually a third court decision out there, from the Third Circuit that suggests a different answer. In this case, *Sebastian Int'l v. Consumer Contacts (PTY) Ltd.*, the court was somewhat reluctant to accept the limitation of the First Sale doctrine only to products manufactured in the U.S. The court also expressed concern about courts unilaterally strengthening copyright protections to address the issues raised by "gray markets."

Three courts came out three different ways because the language of the law is confusing and it appears to lead to "absurd" results (in the Ninth Circuit's words).

But the Supreme Court doesn't have to impose an absurd result on the nation. The first-sale doctrine reflects basic common sense—and follows from the logic of treating copyrights and other "intellectual property" with no more protection than regular property. Ever since the end of Medieval feudalism, and the writings of John Locke, we have understood the importance of being able to buy and sell one's own property, including books and watches, both for reasons of economics and liberty.

The Court has several legal justifications for reaching the right result. Courts are supposed to interpret laws to avoid "absurd results" and to avoid constitutional problems—such as infringing on the free speech rights of Americans that want to buy and sell their own books and creative works that are published abroad and taking away the property rights, without compensation, of the millions of Americans who buy and sell their own stuff every day, in person and online.

Ultimately the Court must choose between bringing copyright law into the Internet age or consigning us all to the dark ages. I hope they choose wisely.

"The copyright industry wants you to 'licence' all your music, your movies your games—and lose your rights to sell them or modify them as you see fit."

Selling Used Digital Goods Is Protected by the First-Sale Doctrine

Corynne McSherry

Corynne McSherry is director of intellectual property at the Electronic Frontier Foundation. In the following viewpoint, McSherry suggests that legal precedents are being set that could destroy the protections of first-sale doctrine. She reviews the Kirtsaeng v. Wiley & Sons *Supreme Court case, which could ruin the used goods market and give businesses incentive to move their manufacturing overseas. McSherry also outlines the case Capitol Records has brought against digital music reseller Redigi. The ruling of this case could tip the power of ownership toward companies rather than consumers. Ultimately, McSherry concludes, copyright industries are seeking to get around first-sale doctrine through licensing, which is a losing proposition for consumers.*

Reselling Digital Music Is Not File Sharing

[ReDigi] allows music lovers to recycle and resell their digital music.... It's not about file sharing, but a legal alternative by verifying the iTunes music was lawfully purchased by the person wanting to resell it before that user's "one and only copy" is uploaded to the cloud for storage.

Darlene Storm, Security Is Sexy *(blog),* Computerworld, *February 9, 2012. http://blogs.computerworld.com.*

As you read, consider the following questions:

1. What section of the Copyright Act outlines the principal idea of the first-sale doctrine, according to McSherry?

2. According to the author, why does Capitol Records object to Redigi's business?

3. In the opinion of McSherry, why is licensing bad for consumers but good for businesses?

The "first sale" doctrine expresses one of the most important limitations on the reach of copyright law. The idea, set out in Section 109 of the Copyright Act, is simple: once you've acquired a lawfully-made CD or book or DVD, you can lend, sell, or give it away without having to get permission from the copyright owner. In simpler terms, "you bought it, you own it" (and because first sale also applies to gifts, "they gave it to you, you own it" is also true).

Seems obvious, right? After all, without the "first sale" doctrine, libraries would be illegal, as would used bookstores, used record stores, etc.

Copyright Owners Dislike the First-Sale Doctrine

But the copyright industries have never liked first sale, since it creates competition for their titles (you could borrow the book from a friend, pick it up at a library, or buy it from a used book seller on Amazon). It also reduces their ability to impose restrictions on how you use the work after it is sold.

Two legal cases now pending could determine the future of the doctrine. The first is *Kirtsaeng v. Wiley & Sons*. In that case, a textbook publisher is trying to undercut first sale by claiming the law only covers goods made in the United States. That would mean anything that is made in a foreign country and contains copies of copyrighted material—from the textbooks at issue in the Kirtsaeng case to shampoo bottles with copyrighted labels—could be blocked from resale, lending, or gifting without the permission of the copyright owner. That would create a nightmare for consumers and businesses, upending used goods markets and undermining what it really means to "buy" and "own" physical goods. The ruling also creates a perverse incentive for U.S. businesses to move their manufacturing operations abroad. It is difficult for us to imagine this is the outcome Congress intended. [The Supreme Court ruled in June 2013 that foreign-made goods fall under the first-sale doctrine, too.—ed.]

Capitol v. Redigi

The second is *Capitol v. Redigi*. Redigi is a service that allows music fans to store and resell music they buy from iTunes. Here's how it works: customers download Redigi software and designate files they want to resell. Redigi's software checks to make sure the files came from iTunes (so it knows they were lawfully purchased), pulls the data files from the reseller's computer to cloud storage, and deletes them from the reseller's hard drive. Once the music is in the cloud, other Redigi users can buy it. When a purchase is made, Redigi transfers ownership of the file and the seller can no longer access it. At last, a way for users to exercise their traditional right to resell music they no longer want.

No way, says Capitol Records. According to Capitol, the first sale doctrine simply doesn't apply to digital goods, because there is no way to "transfer" them without making copies. When users upload their music to the cloud, they are making a copy of that music, whether or not they subsequently (or simultaneously) delete it from their own computers, and the first sale doctrine doesn't protect copying.

A win for Capitol would be profoundly dangerous for consumers. Many of us "buy" music, movies, books, games etc. in purely digital form, and this is likely to be increasingly true going forward. But if Capitol has its way, the laws we count on to protect our right to dispose of that content will be as obsolete as the VHS tape. [The case was still undecided as of this volume's publication.—ed.]

Licensing Skirts the First-Sale Doctrine

The *Redigi* case also highlights another growing problem. Not only does big content deny that first sale doctrine applies to digital goods, but they are also trying to undermine the first sale rights we do have by forcing users to license items they would rather buy. The copyright industry wants you to "license" all your music, your movies, your games—and lose your rights to sell them or modify them as you see fit. These "end user license agreements" reinforce the short-sighted policies that prevent us from lending ebooks to friends, re-selling software packages, or using text-to-speech to read ebooks aloud.

We have been worried about the future of first sale for a long time, but it seems we are reaching a new crisis point. We need to be prepared to tell elected lawmakers that we stand up for first sale, whether the threat comes from arcane import regulations, dangerous legal interpretations, or onerous End

User License Agreements. EFF [Electronic Frontier Foundation] has joined Demand Progress and the Free Software Foundation in giving you a platform to contact your legislators to urge them to stand up for first sale. Take action today.

Periodical and Internet Sources Bibliography

The following articles have been selected to supplement the diverse views presented in this chapter.

Leigh Beadon	"50 Cent Sued over Infringing Sample; When Will Hip-Hop's Stars Speak Up About Copyright?," *Techdirt* (blog), April 23, 2012. www.techdirt.com.
Todd Bishop	"Amazon Wins Broad Patent on Reselling and Lending 'Used' Digital Goods," *GeekWire*, February 4, 2013. www.geekwire.com.
Annemarie Bridy	"The Digital Death of Copyright's First Sale Doctrine," *Freedom to Tinker* (blog), October 10, 2011. https://freedom-to-tinker.com.
Ernesto	"Piracy Is NOT Theft: Problems of a Nonsense Metaphor," *TorrentFreak*, November 4, 2011. http://torrentfreak.com.
Parker Higgins	"Your Right to Own, Under Threat," Electronic Frontier Foundation, October 28, 2012. www.eff.org.
John S. Pelletier	"Sampling the Circuits: The Case for a New Comprehensive Scheme for Determining Copyright Infringement as a Result of Music Sampling," *Washington University Law Review*, vol. 89, no. 5, 2012. lawreview.wustl.edu.
Alan Wexelblat	"On the Used and Pirate Markets for Digital Goods," *Copyfight* (blog), Corante, February 14, 2013. http://copyfight.corante.com.
Marcus Wohlsen	"Amazon Wants to Get Into the Used E-Book Business—or Bury It," *Wired*, February 8, 2013. www.wired.com.

CHAPTER 2

What Is the Economic Impact of Copyright Infringement?

Chapter Preface

The relationship between copyright infringement and the economy is complex and cannot be reduced to a simple cause-and-effect between infringers and lost sales. The parallel changes in digital media and even digital cash flow only add to the complexity. Theories about the effect of infringement upon the economy are fraught with controversy, with many reports claiming numbers that are contradicted by the opposing side, with no clarity as to who might be right. The April 2010 US Government Accountability Office report, "Intellectual Property: Observations on Efforts to Quantify the Economic Effects of Counterfeit and Pirated Goods," concluded that piracy and counterfeit are "sizable" issues, but due to a lack of unbiased research, most people are operating by assumption and bias rather than empirical data.

Music piracy was the frontier of digital infringement. In the 1990s, a combination of personal computers and digital recordings on compact disc (CD) made it easy for people to copy music to their hard drives to listen to, make music mixes of, trade with friends, or even trade over the Internet. Movies followed this trend despite the introduction of Digital Rights Management (DRM), a form of protection embedded on the CDs and DVDs that made it impossible for many people to copy them. New film releases were (and still are) often made available via peer-to-peer networks within days of a film's theatrical release—and the more popular the release, the more often it is shared and downloaded. The music and movie industries have been fighting an uphill battle ever since, leaving many people to wonder whether taking down illegal downloaders entirely is cost effective or even possible.

The latecomer to digital infringement is books. As digital e-readers became both more affordable and more popular in the early twenty-first century, infringement of e-books soared exponentially, according to Matt Frisch, writing for CNN.com in January 2010. For example, Frisch notes, a new novel by Dan Brown saw its e-book edition far outsell its hardcover edition on the first day of release—and within days it had been downloaded illegally from peer-to-peer networks a hundred thousand times. Nonetheless, Brown's novel was still a best seller by conventional measurements, being on the *New York Times* hardcover fiction best-seller list for twenty-nine weeks (more than seven months).

Textbooks, with their high price tags and short shelf life, are an industry niche that appears particularly prone to infringement as students seek alternatives to purchasing books they *must* have, but only for a few months. NetNames.com conducted a nonscientific study of the twenty best-selling textbooks on Amazon.com and found that all but one was widely available as a free e-book on a linking web site that aggregates sources for infringed content. The one book that was not available as a free e-book was, however, available as a free audio book download.

Many publishers and distributors are fighting piracy by being better businesses. Suw Charman-Anderson, writing for *Forbes* in February 2013, argues that digital piracy is never going away and publishers need to stop fighting it tooth-and-nail and instead put their energy into marketing strategies and business models that make legitimate e-books more attractive to consumers. Research has shown that many infringers are everyday people who either do not understand that what they are doing is illegal or they are circumstantial infringers who turn to piracy when the content they seek is not easily available through common venues or is prohibitively expensive.

Some strategies that businesses are using to prevent infringement include e-book lending programs, providing the first book in a series for free download, exclusive supplemental material, and broad access subscriptions. Charman-Anderson suggests that publishers and authors develop closer relationships with readers and offer exclusive merchandise or boxed sets to encourage purchases. Despite the naysayers who claim e-books promote infringement by being so easy to copy, Frisch notes that there is evidence that e-reader owners may buy more books than those who read in the traditional paper format—as much as three to one—which is a boon to an industry struggling to adjust to the changing medium and how it is consumed.

As Charman-Anderson points out, the publishing industry has changed and, for better or worse, there is no turning back. Businesses must adapt or die. Whether or not these changes are hurting the overall economy and the livelihood of people who make their income in publishing is a complex debate that may never be settled before the industry stabilizes again and the argument becomes a matter of historical interest rather than current news. The writers of the viewpoints in the following chapter debate the economic impact of copyright infringement.

> *"The theft or piracy of copyrighted films, television shows, theatrical productions, and music costs the U.S. entertainment industries billions of dollars in revenue each year."*

Copyright Infringement Hurts the Economy

Department for Professional Employees

The Department for Professional Employees (DPE), part of the American Federation of Labor—Congress of Industrial Organizations (AFL-CIO), is a coalition of national unions that represents more than 4 million professional and technical employees in the United States. In the following viewpoint, the DPE argues that protecting and enforcing copyright is crucial for keeping people who support copyrighted industries employed. The DPE details the economic impact of such industries as music, sports, theater, movie and television arts, and museums, as well as secondary businesses, like stores that sell movies and music. The DPE points to the numbers published by the Government Accounting Office as empirical evidence of the damage piracy does to jobs and industries.

As you read, consider the following questions:

1. How many US states have film and television production activity, according to the DPE?

2. According to the author, how much money did the US economy lose to piracy in 2005?

3. How many US jobs were lost in 2005 as a result of film piracy, according to the DPE?

The motion picture, television, theater, and music industries are vital sectors of the U.S. economy. They employ millions of U.S. workers, generate revenues for local businesses and communities, and are among the all-too-few U.S. industries that generate substantial trade surpluses in the midst of growing U.S. trade deficits. The theft or piracy of copyrighted films, television shows, theatrical productions, and music costs the U.S. entertainment industries billions of dollars in revenue each year. That loss of revenue hits directly at bottom-line profits and those who earn their living in these industries. This [viewpoint] examines the consequences of intellectual property (IP) theft for the entertainment industries, their workers, and those in related industries.

Creative Workers and Copyright Must Be Protected

Creative workers rely on copyright protection and royalty or residual payments to make a living from their artistic creations and performances. Even creative workers who are paid for work for hire ultimately rely on the copyright protections of the organizations that pay them. Technology is rapidly changing the way in which consumers enjoy arts and entertainment. Performing and craft professionals in the arts, entertainment, and media, and their unions must work to insure that these professionals are properly compensated.

Copyright is important to creative workers because it grants certain rights and protections in their artistic creations. Copyright provides the basis on which creative workers are compensated for the use of their work.

Copyright is "a form of protection provided by the laws of the United States to the authors of 'original works of authorship,' including literary, dramatic, musical, artistic, and certain other intellectual works." This protection is secured automatically when the work is created and endures for a certain term. Under copyright laws, the holder of the copyright has the exclusive rights to do and authorize others to:

- Reproduce the work in copies;

- Prepare derivative works based on the original work;

- Distribute copies of the work for public sale or other transfer of ownership, or by rental, lease or lending; and

- Display or perform the work publicly or in the case of sound recordings, to perform the work publicly by means of digital audio transmission.

Copyright gives the author control over intellectual property, including the right to distribute a copyrighted work. The copyright holder is able to collect money by licensing others to reproduce, make derivative works from, distribute, perform, or display the copyrighted material.

Creative Workers Should Be Compensated

Creative workers and entertainment professionals often earn a living on copyrighted materials by receiving residual payments. Residuals are "compensation paid for the reuse of" a performer or writer's work in a produced material, like a motion picture, television program, or sound recording. When an entertainment professional receives credit on a produced material, the entertainment professional may be entitled to compensation if the material is used beyond its original exhibition. For example, residual payments begin for an accredited worker on a TV production, "once the show starts re-airing or is released on video, pay television, broadcast TV or basic cable."

Creative workers also earn a living on copyrighted sound recordings through the receipt of royalties from the sale and distribution and the public performance of their creative work.

Unfortunately, not all countries respect copyright laws. To improve copyright protections around the world, the United Nations (UN) created a specialized agency, the World Intellectual Property Organization (WIPO) to promote intellectual property protection through greater cooperation and collaboration among states and international organizations.

Entertainment Industries Are Important to the US Economy

The entertainment industries are a thriving, if often overlooked, part of the U.S. economy.

In 2010, the U.S. Department of Commerce reported that performing arts, spectator sports, museums, and related activities were a value added to the U.S. economy, generating $80.4 billion (0.6 percent of Gross Domestic Product [GDP]). The motion picture and sound recording industries were value added to the U.S. economy, generating $58.4 billion to the nation's GDP in 2010. The performing arts, spectator sports, museums, and related activities employed 543,000 full and part-time employees in 2010. In addition, the motion picture and sound recording industries employed 374,000 full and part-time employees.

Nationally, there are 668,267 businesses in the U.S. involved in the creation or distribution of the arts. They represent 4.05 percent of all businesses. They employ 2.9 million people, or 2.18 percent of all U.S. jobs.

The entertainment industries are a huge employer. In 2010, there were over 2.7 million people employed in arts, design, entertainment, sports, and media occupations. This does not include the many persons employed in retail and other "downstream" or "secondary" industries (movie rental stores, music stores, etc.) that also depend on the entertainment industries.

In addition to being a thriving part of the U.S. economy, the entertainment industries are also some of the most densely unionized industries in the U.S. The largest labor federation in the United States, the American Federation of Labor—Congress of Industrial Organizations (AFL-CIO), has many unions that represent professionals in a host of capacities in the entertainment industries. Among them are Actors' Equity Association (AEA), the American Federation of Musicians (AFM), the American Federation of Television and Radio Artists (AFTRA), the American Guild of Musical Artists (AGMA), the International Alliance of Theatrical Stage Employees, Moving Picture Technicians, Artists and Allied Crafts (IATSE), the International Brotherhood of Electrical Workers (IBEW), the Office and Professional Employees International Union (OPEIU), the Screen Actors Guild (SAG), and the Writers Guild of America, East (WGAE).

Film and TV Production Supports Small Businesses and Communities

Motion picture and television production has an economic impact that extends far beyond what is seen onscreen, and offers a concrete example of broad economic benefits. The U.S. motion picture and television industry is a jobs engine nationwide, employing millions of U.S. workers, and supporting numerous small businesses and entrepreneurs.

The U.S. motion picture and television industry is an important contributor to the U.S. economy, with an $11.9 billion trade surplus in 2009 and employing 2.2 million people. The motion picture and television industry employs not only ac-

Copyright Infringement May Slow U.S. Economy

The U.S. economy as a whole may grow at a slower pace than it otherwise would because of counterfeiting and piracy's effect on U.S. industries, government, and consumers. According to officials we interviewed and OECD's 2008 study, to the extent that companies experience a loss of revenues or incentives to invest in research and development for new products, slower economic growth could occur. IP-related industries play an important role in the growth of the U.S. economy and contribute a significant percentage to the U.S. gross domestic product. IP-related industries also pay significantly higher wages than other industries and contribute to a higher standard of living in the United States. To the extent that counterfeiting and piracy reduce investments in research and development, these companies may hire fewer workers and may contribute less to U.S. economic growth, overall. The U.S. economy may also experience slower growth due to a decline in trade with countries where widespread counterfeiting hinders the activities of U.S. companies operating overseas.

In addition to the industry effects, the U.S. economy, as a whole, also may experience effects of losses by consumers and government. An economy's gross domestic product could be measured as either the total expenditures by households (consumers), or as the total wages paid by the private sector (industry). Hence, the effect of counterfeiting and piracy on industry would affect consumers by reducing their wages, which could reduce consumption of goods and services and the gross domestic product. Finally, the government is also affected by the reduction of economic activity, since fewer taxes are collected.

US Government Accountability Office, Intellectual Property: Observations on Efforts to Quantify the Economic Effects of Counterfeit and Pirated Goods, *April 2010.*

tors, writers, and craftspeople on set, but also generates vital secondary industries, like movie theater staff, video rental operations, costume dry cleaners, and on-set caterers.

In 2009, the movie and television industry made $38.9 billion in payments to U.S. vendors, suppliers, small businesses, and entrepreneurs. That same year the industry paid $40.5 billion in wages to American workers.

The economic impact of the motion picture and television industry extends far beyond California and New York. All fifty states and the District of Columbia have activity in film and television production, providing jobs and business to local communities.

Defending U.S. Jobs by Combating Piracy

The broad reach of the entertainment and copyright industries means that digital theft and counterfeiting hurt average American workers and the U.S. government.

A 2010 report by the Government Accountability Office (GAO), *Intellectual Property [IP]: Observations on Efforts to Quantify the Economic Effects of Counterfeit and Pirated Goods*, reviews the literature measuring the effects of IP theft on a range of goods and services, from media to pharmaceuticals. The GAO finds that data measuring the economic impacts of piracy are difficult to obtain and hard to quantify; however, it is clear that IP theft has significant negative effects on consumers, the arts and entertainment industries, as well as the government.

The GAO finds that IP theft and counterfeiting in some industries (pharmaceuticals, for example) may negatively affect consumers by compromising their health and safety, as well as provide the consumer with lower quality goods.

The GAO also found that the arts and entertainment industries incur losses on sales of products like CDs and DVDs as a result of IP theft and that the low quality of pirated goods can damage a brand or artist's value and image. Arts and entertainment businesses incur increased costs trying to protect intellectual property which, coupled with a loss of sales from piracy, decreases the incentives for companies to invest in research and development and new production.

The government is also negatively affected by IP theft. The government is responsible for the cost of enforcing all U.S. intellectual property laws while losing tax revenue that would have been generated by the sale of non-pirated goods.

Piracy Damages the Entertainment Industry

The GAO study finds that no single calculation is effective for accurately measuring revenue and job loss as a result of copyright infringement and counterfeit production. The estimates developed by several organizations monitoring IP theft, however, offer a picture of the negative impact that these practices have on the motion picture, television, theatre, and music industries and the professionals who work in them. While these studies may have flaws, they provide a sense of the magnitude of the economic effects of intellectual property theft.

In 2005, the Organization of Economic Co-operation and Development (OECD) estimated that the international trade in counterfeit and pirated products was approximately $200 billion. This estimate does not include domestically produced and consumed counterfeit and pirated products or those pirated products distributed via the Internet. The OECD reports that if these items were calculated the total magnitude of counterfeiting and digital theft worldwide would be several hundred billion dollars more.

To put these numbers in perspective, in 2005 the international trade of counterfeit and pirated goods (approximately $200 billion) was larger than the national GDP of 150 countries.

The U.S. Trade Representative estimated that the U.S. economy lost between $200 and $250 billion in 2005 due to piracy.

IP theft has a negative effect on employment in all copyright industries. It is estimated that the U.S. economy loses 373,375 jobs annually due to piracy.

In addition, U.S. workers lose $16.3 billion in earnings annually as a result of copyright piracy. Broken down, $7.2 billion in earnings would have gone to workers in the copyright industries or in downstream retail industries and $9.1 billion in earnings would have gone to workers in other U.S. industries.

Music Piracy Leads to Lost Jobs

The music industry has been deeply hurt by the increase in recent years of digital sound recording theft. In 2005, the U.S. economy lost an estimated $12.5 billion in total output due to music piracy.

Music piracy cost the U.S. economy an estimated 71,060 jobs in both the sound recording industry and downstream retail industries. In addition, music piracy cost U.S. workers $2.7 billion in earnings.

Music piracy also results in lost tax revenue for U.S. federal, state, and local governments totaling an estimated $422 million in 2005.

The International Federation of the Phonographic Industry (IFPI) estimated in 2005 that 1.2 billion pirated CDs were purchased that year and, even at reduced pirate prices, the worldwide pirated CD market could be valued at $4.5 billion.

Motion Picture Piracy Reduces Tax Revenues

Like the music industry, the motion picture industry has been adversely affected by piracy. In 2005, worldwide motion picture piracy had an estimated loss of $20.5 billion in output annually.

Motion picture piracy has an effect on employment both in the motion picture industry and in industries related to or that do business with the motion picture industry. In 2005, piracy in motion pictures cost the U.S. economy an estimated 141,030 jobs. Employees in motion picture and related industries lost an estimated $1.903 billion in earnings as a result of motion picture piracy. About two-thirds of these losses were for U.S. workers in industries outside of the motion picture production and retail industries.

Losses from motion picture piracy also result in lower tax revenues for state and local governments. It is estimated that in 2005, motion picture piracy cost U.S. federal, state and local governments $837 million in tax revenues.

Piracy Reaches Live Theatre

No part of the entertainment industries is immune from the adverse impact of intellectual property theft. Live theatre, for example, has begun to be "cinecast" or shown in movie theatres to expand the number of audiences able to take in stage performances. This then opens stage productions to the same tactics IP thieves use to pirate motion pictures, which, again, results in a loss of income to the producers, artists, and craftspeople. While the piracy of captured live performance is unlikely to shut down the live performance, it still has an impact on the earnings of all involved.

"On the data available so far ... reports
of the death of the [copyright] industry
seem much exaggerated."

The Negative Economic Effects of Copyright Infringement Are Overstated

Julian Sanchez

Julian Sanchez is a writer who specializes in technology and politics. He is a research fellow for the Cato Institute and contributing editor to Reason *magazine. In the following viewpoint, Sanchez contends that the industry hype about digital piracy and the need to legislate against it is a problem that is being overstated in economic terms. Sanchez points out that the copyrighted industries—including music, television, and movie production—are weathering the recession of the early twenty-first century better than most industries. For example, he points out, consumers are shifting their music spending to concerts rather than albums, but they are still spending on music overall. Ultimately, Sanchez writes, the economic losses due to piracy are so small compared to the costs of combatting piracy—paid by taxpayers in the event of a legislative solution—that it makes no sense for Congress to spend so much time on this issue.*

As you read, consider the following questions:

1. According to Sanchez, how many new album releases were there in 2010?

2. Why does the author argue that worrying about movie piracy should be a small problem for film-production houses?

3. According to Sanchez, why is it inaccurate to use jobs-effects estimates from a 2007 study to examine the economic impact of digital piracy?

Earlier this month [January 2012], I detailed at some length why claims about the purported economic harms of piracy, offered by supporters of the Stop Online Piracy Act (SOPA) and PROTECT-IP Act (PIPA), ought to be treated with much more skepticism than they generally get from journalists and policymakers. My own view is that this ought to be rather secondary to the policy discussion: SOPA and PIPA would be ineffective mechanisms for addressing the problem, and a terrible idea for many other reasons, even if the numbers were exactly right. No matter how bad last season's crops were, witch burnings are a poor policy response. Fortunately, legislators finally seem to be cottoning on to this: SOPA now appears to be on ice for the time being, and PIPA's own sponsors are having second thoughts about mucking with the Internet's Domain Name System.

Unwarranted Hype

That said, I remain a bit amazed that it's become an indisputable premise in Washington that there's an enormous piracy problem, that it's having a devastating impact on U.S. content industries, and that *some* kind of aggressive new legislation is needed *tout suite* [right away] to stanch the bleeding. Despite the fact that the Government Accountability Office [GAO] recently concluded that it is "difficult, if not impossible, to quantify the net effect of counterfeiting and piracy on the economy as a whole," our legislative class has somehow determined that—among all the dire challenges now facing the United States—*this* is an urgent priority. Obviously, there's quite a lot of copyrighted material circulating on the Internet without authorization, and other things [being] equal, one would like to see less of it. But does the best available evidence show that this is inflicting such catastrophic economic harm—that it is depressing so much output, and destroying so many jobs—that Congress has no option but to Do Something immediately? Bearing the GAO's warning in mind, the data we *do* have doesn't remotely seem to justify the DEFCON One [highest level of defense readiness] rhetoric that now appears to be obligatory on the Hill.

Weathering the Recession Just Fine

The International Intellectual Property Alliance—a kind of meta-trade association for all the content industries, and a zealous prophet of the piracy apocalypse, released a report back in November [2011] meant to establish that copyright industries are so economically valuable that they merit more vigorous government protection. But it actually paints a picture of industries that, far from being "killed" by piracy, are *already* weathering a harsh economic climate better than most, and have far outperformed the overall U.S. economy through the current recession. The "core copyright industries" have, unsurprisingly, shed some jobs over the past few years, but again, compared with the rest of the economy, employment seems to have held relatively stable at a time when you might expect cash-strapped consumers to be turning to piracy to save money.

Music and Movie Releases Are Increasing

Since the core function of copyright is to incentivize the production of creative works, it's also worth looking for signs of declining output associated with filesharing. Empirically, it's surprisingly hard to find an effect. Rather, a recent [2010] survey study by Felix Oberholzer-Gee of the Harvard Business School concluded that "data on the supply of new works are consistent with the argument that file sharing did not discourage authors and publishers" from producing more works, at least in the U.S. market.

So, for instance, Nielsen SoundScan data shows new album releases stood at 35,516 in 2000, peaked at 106,000 in 2008, and (amidst a general recession) fell back to mid-decade levels of about 75,000 for 2010. That's against a general background of falling sales since 2004—mostly explained by factors unrelated to piracy—which finally seems to have reversed in 2011. The actual picture is probably somewhat better than that, because SoundScan data are markedly incomplete when it comes to the releases by indie artists who've benefited most from the rise of digital distribution.

If we look at movies, the numbers compiled by the industry statistics site Box Office Mojo show an average of 558 releases from American studios over the past decade, which rises to 578 if you focus on just the past five years. The average for the *previous* decade—before illicit movie downloads were even an option on most people's radar—is 472 releases per year. (As we learn from a recent Congressional Research Service report, it's weirdly hard to detect a strong overall correlation between output and employment in the motion picture industry, which actually fell slightly from 1998 to 2008, even as profits and CEO [chief executive officer] pay soared. One reason the growing trend in recent decades for "Hollywood" features to actually be produced in Canada or Australia.)

Consumers Spending More on Concerts

That's all very nice, one might object, but wouldn't these heartening numbers be *even higher* if labels and studios could recapture some of the revenue lost to illicit downloads? Well, they surely *might*—but it's not nearly as clear as you'd think.

One reason is that they already *are* recapturing much of that revenue through "complementary" purchases. As Oberholzer-Gee observes, recording industry numbers show large increases in concert revenues corresponding to the drop in recorded music sales. That suggests that, as people discover new artists by sampling downloaded albums online, they're shifting consumption *within* the sector to live performances. In other words, people have a roughly constant "music budget," and what they don't spend on the albums they've downloaded gets spent on seeing that new band they discovered. For the firms that specifically make their money from the sale of recordings, that may seem like cold comfort, but if we're concerned with the *music* industry as a whole, it's a wash. Something similar might occur with respect to purchases of merchandise based on licensed film properties.

Successful Films Are Being Pirated

Another factor is that, notwithstanding projections of a "long tail" effect resulting from lower search and distribution costs in the digital era, most entertainment industries continue to operate on a "tournament" or "lottery" model, where a few hits generate jackpot revenues, sufficient to make up for losses on the majority of new products. Unsurprisingly, the most heavily pirated movies each year tend to be the ones that are also highly successful at the box office and in DVD sales, with similar patterns in album downloads. In other words, bleeding revenue to piracy is going to be a problem to the extent that your product is a hit, in a market where the core uncertainty about this crucial fact (at the time when the decision whether to greenlight production is made) looms a lot larger than the marginal loss from illicit downloads if you *are* successful.

It's a tricky but more or less tractable problem to estimate roughly how many full-time jobs you'll need regionally to support one additional $150 million movie production next year. It's a totally different question how aggregate sectoral employment in a volatile and evolving industry changes based on investor responses to a $150 million across-the-board drop in the size of the total film jackpot, especially given that arcane financial arrangements are one place Hollywood does show a genius for constantly adapting its business model. If you want to know how many people are getting laid off when McDonald's revenues drop, it makes a difference whether it's each of 13,000 franchises earning $100 less per year, or one franchise earning $1.3 million less, even though the total reduction is the same.

A Glut of Movies

Finally, *more demand for content* being captured by the content industries is not always the same thing as *demand for more content*, in the sense of "a greater variety of output." I noted earlier that the past few years have seen a significant spike in the number of movie titles released annually. But as the *Los Angeles Times* reported in 2008, studio executives soon began complaining about a "glut" of new movies, many of which were targeted at the same demographics, and therefore cannibalizing their own audiences. As one executive suggested, that meant that (at least in a market dominated by a few huge distributors) releasing *fewer* titles could yield higher profits—and, indeed, the number of titles released in the following two years dropped back to mid-decade levels. The key point here is that shifting some portion of the pirate audience to some form of legal viewing doesn't necessarily change this basic calculus, because there's an upper bound to the number of hours most people are going to spend watching (say) racing movies, whether they're paying for the privilege or not. Rising demand can just as easily, for instance, bid up star salaries for a fixed number of films.

Digital Economics Are Weirder

The point here isn't that piracy by American consumers is somehow completely independent from output or employment rates in the content industries—though, again, that's not at all the same thing as the *overall U.S. employment rate.* Obviously, at *some* level it has to have some effect. But the link is, to use the technical economic term, *weirder* than in many other sectors of the economy. In many industries, the relationship between consumer spending and job creation is *relatively* straightforward. If demand for widgets or restaurant meals rises, satisfying that demand requires a roughly linear increase in widget factories and restaurants, in hiring of widget-makers and cooks and waiters, and in purchases of the raw material inputs for those goods. Distribution of copyrighted content—and in particular digital distribution over the Internet—is a bit more complicated, for precisely the same reason piracy is an issue: once the first copy of a work has been created, an unlimited number of additional units (of the digital product) can be produced at effectively zero cost.

Reducing Piracy Would Matter Little

Let's imagine, implausibly, that a measure like SOPA *did* manage to reduce online piracy by U.S. consumers by some meaningful amount. A small portion of that reduction, the minority of downloads representing legal purchases displaced by file sharing, would translate into sales for the content industries. What form would these take? It seems reasonable to suppose that the majority of people who were previously getting their music and movies from The Pirate Bay are not typically lining up to buy shiny plastic discs at Wal-Mart. Rather, they're probably disproportionately displacing *legal digital downloads* from venues like iTunes and Amazon, or subscription services like Netflix and Spotify, which are pretty clearly where the overall market is quickly going anyway. (Apparently, literal thieves don't even bother stealing physical media anymore.)

For movies, there's probably also some displacement of theatrical ticket sales, though as the theatrical experience is in many ways a distinct good, it's hard to say how much substitution it's reasonable to expect.

Online vs. Brick-and-Mortar Economics

In the very short term, increased legal purchases of digital content wouldn't seem likely to generate many additional jobs. If spending in the physical retail sector jumps 20 percent, shops need to hire more clerks, and their suppliers more manufacturing workers, to meet the increased demand. If spending in the iTunes store jumps 20 percent, Apple probably needs to pay a few bucks more for bandwidth and electricity, but basically everyone just gets to smile and pocket the extra profit. The jobs effects estimates we're seeing tossed around, however, are coming from a 2007 study that would have had to employ, at the most recent, adjustments made several years before *that* to the benchmark multipliers the Bureau of Economic Analysis developed in 2002. Even leaving aside its many other problems, then, the job impact estimates in that study would have been largely based on legacy assumptions from a brick-and-mortar economy. (The loss estimates relied on would also, necessarily, fail to account for the recent rise of popular, legal streaming services that have likely lured many consumers back from the pirate market. There is, alas, no very good data here, but I'd wager Hulu and Netflix have done exponentially more to reduce piracy losses than enforcement crackdowns ever will.) In any event, you'd expect the most *immediate* effect of consumer spending shifts from widgets and restaurants to digital downloads would be, if anything, fewer *net* jobs. The output and employment effects, rather, would show up in the longer term as lower returns reduce incentives to produce new content—and hire the workers needed to support that production. For some of the reasons discussed above, though, empirically there's just not much evidence for a dramatic effect of this kind.

Not Worth the Cost

No doubt piracy is costing the content industries *some-thing*—or they wouldn't be throwing so much money at Congress in support of this kind of legislation. If we could wave a magic wand and have less piracy, obviously that would be good. But in the real world, where enforcement has direct costs to the taxpayer, regulation has costs on the industries it burdens, and the reduction in piracy they're likely to produce is very small, it seems important to point out that the credible evidence for the *magnitude* of the harm is fairly thin. As a rough analogy, since antipiracy crusaders are fond of equating filesharing with shoplifting: suppose the CEO of Wal-Mart came to Congress demanding a $50 million program to deploy FBI agents to frisk suspicious-looking teens in towns near Wal-Marts. A lawmaker might, without for one instant doubting that shoplifting is a bad thing, question whether this is really the optimal use of federal law enforcement resources. The CEO indignantly points out that shoplifting *kills one million adorable towheaded orphans* each year. The proof is right here in this study by the Wal-Mart Institute for Anti-Shoplifting Studies. The study sources this dramatic claim to a newspaper article, which quotes the CEO of Wal-Mart asserting (on the basis of private data you can't see) that shoplifting kills hundreds of orphans annually. And as a footnote explains, it seemed prudent to round up to a million. I wish this were *just* a joke, but . . . that's literally about the level of evidence we're dealing with here.

In short, piracy is certainly one problem in a world filled with problems. But politicians and journalists seem to have been persuaded to take it largely on faith that it's a uniquely dire and pressing problem that demands dramatic remedies with little time for deliberation. On the data available so far, though, reports of the death of the industry seem much exaggerated.

> *"There is ample reason to believe that a non-zero level of copyright infringement is socially beneficial."*

Why Should We Stop Online Piracy?

Matthew Yglesias

Matthew Yglesias is the business and economic correspondent for Slate *magazine. In the following viewpoint, Yglesias describes how digital piracy functions as a solution to economic deadweight loss of consumers who would not otherwise consume the content they download. This is in part due to what consumers regard as the high cost of digital goods that Yglesias points out can be reproduced almost infinitely at little cost to the manufacturer. Lack of access to available products also creates an underground market, Yglesias argues, and illustrates his point with an example from a popular BBC television show. His final point drives home that innovation, creativity, and output are clearly not suffering in the American market, so while it is important to maintain that piracy is an illegal activity, it is not worth the effort to heavily legislate against it.*

As you read, consider the following questions:

1. How does Yglesias compare online piracy to basketball?

2. According to Yglesias, what economic function do used bookstores and libraries serve?

3. Why is it important to force copyright industries to compete with the piracy market, according to the author?

Congressional bill names are a reliable indicator of the state of conventional wisdom in America. That Congress is weighing bills called the Stop Online Piracy Act [SOPA] and the Protect IP Act [PIPA] tells us that, at a minimum, the *idea* of stopping online piracy is popular.

It shouldn't be. There's no evidence that the United States is currently suffering from an excessive amount of online piracy, and there is ample reason to believe that a non-zero level of copyright infringement is socially beneficial. Online piracy is like fouling in basketball. You want to penalize it to prevent it from getting out of control, but any effort to actually eliminate it would be a cure much worse than the disease.

Absurdly Inflated Claims

Much of the debate about SOPA and PIPA has thus far centered around the entertainment industry's absurdly inflated claims about the economic harm of copyright infringement. When making these calculations, intellectual property owners tend to assume that every unauthorized download represents a lost sale. This is clearly false. Often people copy a file illegally precisely because they're unwilling to pay the market price. Were unauthorized copying not an option, they would simply not watch the movie or listen to the album.

Critics of industry estimates have repeatedly made this point and argued against the inflated figures used by SOPA and Protect IP boosters. But an equally large problem is the failure to consider the *benefits* to illegal downloading. These benefits can be a simple reduction of what economists call "deadweight loss." Deadweight loss exists any time the profit-maximizing price of a unit of something exceeds the cost of producing an extra unit. In a highly competitive market in which many sellers are offering largely undifferentiated goods, profit margins are low and deadweight loss is tiny. But the whole point of copyright is that the owner of the rights to, say, [the popular TV series] *Breaking Bad* has a monopoly on sales of new episodes of the show. At the same time, producing an extra copy of a *Breaking Bad* episode is nearly free. So when the powers that be decide that the profit-maximizing strategy is to charge more than $100 to download all four seasons of *Breaking Bad* from iTunes, they're creating a situation in which lots of people who'd gain $15 or $85 worth of enjoyment from watching the show can't watch it. This is "deadweight loss," and to the extent that copyright infringement reduces it, infringement is a boon to society.

Pirates Spend Their Money Elsewhere

After all, things like public libraries, used bookstores, and the widespread practice of lending books to friends all cost publishers money. But nobody (I hope) is going to introduce the Stop Used Bookstores Now Act purely on these grounds. The public policy question is not whether the libraries are bad for publishers, but whether libraries are beneficial on *balance.*

By the same token, even when copyright infringement does lead to real loss of revenue to copyright owners, it's not as if the money vanishes into a black hole. Suppose Joe Downloader uses BitTorrent to get a free copy of *Beggars Banquet* rather than forking over $7.99 to Amazon, and then goes out to eat some pizza. In this case, the Rolling Stones' loss is the pizzeria's gain *and* Joe gets to listen to a classic album. It's at least not obvious that we should regard this, on balance, as harmful.

Unavailability Creates a Black Market

Meanwhile, the benefits of forcing copyright holders to compete with free-but-illegal downloads are considerable. I am not, personally, in the habit of infringing on copyrights (though I will cop to some book lending and the fact that my fiancée and I, like any sensible couple, share Netflix and Hulu subscriptions) but recently have found myself firing up btjunkie.org [now shut down] again. Why? Because the BBC [British Broadcasting Corporation] in its infinite wisdom decided to start airing Season 2 of its excellent program *Sherlock* in the United Kingdom without making it available at any price to Americans. That's dumb, but until relatively recently it was a universal problem. It used to be that studios and labels didn't make their wares available to people willing to pay for them. That created an underground market for pirated TV shows and music. The pirated market, in turn, pressured the entertainment industry to create legal options such as iTunes and Hulu. The illegal competition is a valuable consumer pressure on the industry.

Piracy Does Not Suppress Innovation

This is not to say that we should have no copyright law or that there should be no penalties for piracy. Used book stores may slightly depress sales of new books, but they don't threaten to destroy the entire publishing industry. Large-scale, unimpeded, commercialized digital reproduction of other people's works really could destroy America's creative industries. But the question to ask about the state of intellectual property policy is whether there's a problem from the consumer side. If infringement got out of hand, we might face a bleak scenario in which bands stop recording albums and no new TV shows are released.

But we're clearly not living in that world. There are plenty of books to read, things to watch, and music to listen to. Indeed, the American consumer has never been better-entertained than she is today. The same digital frontier that's created the piracy pseudo-problem has created whole new companies and made it infinitely easier for small operations to distribute their products. Digital technology has reduced the price we pay for new works and made them cheaper to create. I can watch a feature film on my telephone.

The American economy has plenty of problems, but lack of adequate entertainment options is not on the list. SOPA isn't just an overly intrusive way to solve a problem, it's a "solution" to a problem that's not a problem.

> "By February 2011 ... more than 100,000 people in the United States were facing allegations of copyright infringement."

Copyright Infringement Litigation Creates Legal and Financial Burdens

Eriq Gardner

Eriq Gardner is a journalist who writes on media and the law. In the following viewpoint, Gardner discusses the copyright trolling company Righthaven, which, he explains, pursued profit through litigation. Righthaven assumed the rights over more than 130 newspapers, Gardner reports, and then slapped lawsuits against small news sources and bloggers who had reposted this material online. Many people chose to settle out of court, Gardner states, but some fought back and eventually Righthaven was closed down when the courts disagreed with the legality of Righthaven's practice and effectively put it out of business. The courts not only found Righthaven's assumption of others' copyrights illegal, Gardner writes, they also determined that the reposting of articles was within the fair-use doctrine most of the time.

As you read, consider the following questions:

1. According to Gardner, to what profit agreement did Righthaven come with the newspapers of which it assumed copyright?

2. How many people did the RIAA go after between 2003 and 2008 for illegal peer-to-peer music sharing, according to the author?

3. According to Gardner, what different ideas have been posited as to why Righthaven was founded and operated as it was, rather than have its lawyers represent the newspapers in a more traditional fashion?

Almost anyone who uses the Internet and is slightly curious about their own digital existence has, over the past decade, had what might be termed a Google moment. These are times, as you type your name into the search engine box, that you realize you don't have control, that whatever you've done in your life is free to be appropriated and contextualized in all sorts of ways. We have identities, and then we have digital identities; and it's not hard, when you're looking through the digital looking glass of a Google ego surf, to wonder which is more important.

My strangest Google moment came one day last year [2011] when Google's search engine monkeys led me to an article in the *Las Vegas Sun* revealing that I had just been sued. The plaintiff in the lawsuit was Righthaven, a company founded in early 2010 with the express purpose of suing copyright infringers on the Internet.

I've written about this company just once before, in a December 2010 article for *Ars Technica* that revealed that the company had picked a new target—the *Drudge Report*. My article included an image from Righthaven's legal papers of a picture the company claimed to own. For this copy of a copy of a copy, I became Righthaven's latest mark.

A Public Relations Maelstrom

From there, Righthaven's ambitions quickly unraveled. A few days later, facing a PR maelstrom for suing a journalist who had written about the company, Righthaven was forced to admit that the filing was "an internal error," a "clerical mistake," something that had happened because the machinery of mass suing lacked a decent check against a reporter's fair use. The lawsuit against me was soon dismissed with prejudice.

Within a couple of months of suing me, Righthaven announced that it had suspended filing new lawsuits.

But the knocks kept coming for the company: court decisions that let defendants use substantial portions of the company's material without penalty, judges who questioned whether Righthaven was properly assigned its claimed copyrighted material, media partners withdrawing their support, and more court decisions that ordered the company to pay legal fees to successful defendants.

By last September [2011], Righthaven had told one Nevada federal judge it was considering filing for bankruptcy. Soon the company's domain name was seized and, rather embarrassingly, auctioned off to satisfy debts.

Now the company's leaders—copyright attorneys responsible for launching more than 250 lawsuits in an amazing 18-month flurry—are being investigated by the State Bar of Nevada for their actions.

And despite all of this, Righthaven CEO Steven Gibson, a partner at Dickinson Wright in Las Vegas, is not only unapologetic about everything that's happened but also still believes the Righthaven experiment will ultimately prove successful.

"Righthaven remains the vehicle for dealing with infringements on the Internet," Gibson told me recently. "Those who write poems, those who create movies, those who want to publish need to have a sense of protectability. If you want to have newspapers survive, protected from aggregators on the

Eloise Sues to Defend Her Work from Infringement

I took legal advice up to the point where I was offered a quote. The $40,000 (£25,000+) bill just to begin court procedures seemed a tad steep to me. I understood then that I could risk going into debt just to defend my intellectual property. I have since also learnt that the legal procedures can be excruciating, as you are treated as a suspect and a possible criminal. There is always the chance that the other party will fight your pockets instead of your evidence by dragging out the procedures and even after you win you are not guaranteed your legal expenses back.

Eloise, interviewed by Amity Roach,
Etsy, *May 21, 2010. www.etsy.com.*

Internet, you've got to think about the vehicle through which that protection can occur. I don't think anyone besides Righthaven has thought about that."

The Example of the *New York Times*

For the past decade, a number of content studios have been experiencing their own Google moments.

They look out and, besides seeing pesky pirates and annoying aggregators, they're bedeviled by a confluence of other factors diminishing the value of being in the content business.

Take the *New York Times*. A decade ago, according to one study by *Business Insider*, the newspaper had $540 million of operating profit. Today, even as its online operations take in more revenue than ever before, that figure has shrunk to just $61 million. Crunching the numbers, the authors of the study concluded that the newspaper's digital business will eventually be able to support a newsroom that's only one-third to one-half its current size.

And so big content businesses, recognizing ongoing distribution and pricing troubles, have been searching for salvation.

Controversial Legislative Efforts

For many, that's meant an attempt to broaden legal protections for content owners. Last winter, Hollywood led an effort to get lawmakers to pass new legislation intended to crack down on foreign "rogue" sites devoted to piracy. The Stop Online Piracy Act [SOPA] and the Protect-IP Act [PIPA] would have allowed the Justice Department and private copyright owners to go to court and, after getting judicial blessing, required U.S.-based websites to make efforts like blocking access to these foreign sites, cutting off support from advertisement and payment processing networks, and eliminating the presence of these foreign sites on search engines. Reaction to the controversial plan slowly escalated until the crescendo of cries reached from all corners of the Internet: Lawmakers were intent on damaging free speech protections and threatening innovation on the Web.

Meanwhile, as some content owners look outward for help, others are attempting to figure out whether there's a more economical way to bolster the old media regime. For many, that includes adapting to the times and coming up with new or better business models. But for a few content owners, in a more agitated state of mind, it's meant taking the existing copyright regime and doing whatever is necessary to survive.

The Righthaven Experiment

That's where Righthaven comes in.

Formed in 2010, the company signed agreements with Stephens Media, publisher of 75 newspapers, including the *Las Vegas Review-Journal*; WEHCO Media, publisher of 10 newspapers; and MediaNews Group, publisher of 56 newspapers, including the *Denver Post* and the *San Jose Mercury News*. Righthaven was assigned limited rights to the copyrights of articles and photographs from these newspapers. In return, Righthaven agreed to share 50 percent of the proceeds from any lawsuit winnings after the deduction of legal costs.

Litigation can be an expensive proposition, however, so Righthaven's legal campaign required some game-planning about the types of targets the company would pursue. Righthaven decided it would be best to ignore both foreign pirates and any large media company that might engage in copyright infringement. Instigating a lengthy court battle or dealing with the vagaries of foreign jurisdictions would not be worth it. Instead, the company appeared to go after small proprietors such as mom-and-pop Web publishers who perhaps were a tad too aggressive in their copying-and-pasting and might bend quickly to a settlement demand.

Pursuing the Weakest Defendants

Just a few months after it was formed, Righthaven was responsible for a tidal wave of copyright infringement lawsuits in the court system. The defendants made good stories, such as a chronically ill, autistic blogger who was slapped with a lawsuit for posting an image from the *Denver Post* of a TSA [Transportation Security Administration] agent doing an airline security pat-down. (This was the same image that would later bite me.)

Along with the lawsuits came settle-or-else demand letters. Righthaven told its defendants that $6,000 would need to be handed over to quash a lawsuit. Many, including the *Drudge Report*, paid up so as to avoid the hassle. Some defendants pleaded poverty. And a few hired lawyers to put up a defense.

Some of those lawyers registered distaste about what was happening and felt compelled to stand up to a bully in their midst.

"Practical lawyering in an area of law I actually like often disgusts me now," wrote one of those attorneys, Ron Coleman, on his blog.

Protecting Intellectual Property

I've been covering media and law for nearly a decade. In that time, I've written about some of the key efforts to use the court system to protect intellectual property from the intrusions of the new digital vanguard.

The Digital Millennium Copyright Act, signed into law by President Bill Clinton in 1998, established protections for digital content, and lawsuits in the aftermath have shaped liability for Internet service providers who host, often unwittingly, copyright infringing material. By now, it's well-established that websites have to respond expeditiously when informed by a copyright holder of misappropriated content, but the reach of the law has had limited effect on the spread of pirated work. Infringements taken down in one spot are often put up in another, and often on foreign websites free of strong statutory obligations.

In reaction to this situation, the content business keeps flirting with the idea that the only way to really make a dent against piracy is to teach the pirates themselves a hard legal lesson by making them pay for their bad acts.

The Righthaven experiment was not the first to go after pirates on a massive scale. From 2003 to 2008, the Recording Industry Association of America [RIAA] took legal action against an estimated 30,000 individuals for sharing music on peer-to-peer platforms like Grokster and Kazaa. The industry group eventually backed down because of the public relations fallout and the enormous expense of the nationwide litigation.

But the idea that mass suing represents a solution to online piracy hasn't died with the RIAA's retreat. Far from it. I know.

A New Approach to Copyright Litigation

In the early months of 2010, an enterprising law firm based in Washington, D.C., began a new effort to sue individuals who had engaged in copyright theft via "torrent websites"—sites that use BitTorrent technology for file sharing. What made the efforts of this firm calling itself the US Copyright Group so unique were its tactics: On behalf of its indie film clients, the firm joined thousands of "John Does" as defendants into a single lawsuit, then got a judge to subpoena ISPs [Internet service providers] for identifying information. Afterward, the alleged pirates, once revealed, would get a settle-or-else demand.

In March 2010, I wrote an article for *The Hollywood Reporter* describing this new legal campaign.

In the months that followed, the mass-joinder litigation started to gather national press attention. Large ISPs like Time Warner Cable resisted subpoenas. Public advocacy groups like the Electronic Frontier Foundation made it a priority to fight the "trolling" threat. And already overburdened judges struggled with the resulting storm of lawsuits.

Other companies soon adopted the tactics of the US Copyright Group, including big book publishers like John Wiley & Sons. The porn industry was able to put its own spin on the litigation with the implicit threat of revealing legal targets who refused to settle as enjoying gay porn, bestiality or other potentially embarrassing entertainments.

By February 2011, less than a year after my story came out about the US Copyright Group, more than 100,000 people in the United States were facing allegations of copyright infringement. Five years ago, during the height of the RIAA's litigation campaign, fewer than 6,000 copyright cases were pending in the courts.

Lawyers Miffed at Righthaven

Though the business of mass suing seems black and white for "copyright maximalists" (those who favor laws conferring broad rights and protections to content creators) and "copy-fighters" (those who prefer looser protections in the name of technological innovation), the ethics of enforcement is a topic that generates some surprising opinions.

Consider Marc Randazza, who is probably the lawyer who has done the most to destroy Righthaven: His court-ordered legal fees for vigorously defending a Righthaven target forced the company to sell its own domain name. (It was purchased by a Switzerland-based company that promised to offer Web-hosting services with "a little more backbone" against legal threats.) Randazza, whose multistate practice is based in Las Vegas, calls what Righthaven did "arrogance beyond belief."

Yet Randazza maintains he is a supporter of the general principles behind SOPA. He says that the research he started a few years ago for a paper attacking the RIAA's mass-suing campaign led him to an opposite conclusion. "I have complete respect for what the RIAA did," he says.

Or take Thomas M. Dunlap, the D.C.-based leader of the US Copyright Group, whose mass-joinder litigation efforts against individual pirates became a legal phenomenon. One might expect him to have sympathy for what Righthaven went through, but he's no fan of the company either. Dunlap says the "biggest mistake they made was not doing their copyright homework."

He's not alone in that feeling.

Righthaven's Gibson tells me that he believes the efforts against his company were led by those whose agenda was to weaken copyright laws. "The same folks battling SOPA were battling Righthaven," Gibson says.

Righthaven Ignored Fair Use Doctrine

But Robert Levine, author of *Free Ride: How Digital Parasites Are Destroying the Culture Business, and How the Culture Business Can Fight Back*, says he believes that Righthaven messed up "a lot of stuff, including the basic idea of giving small players a mechanism to enforce their rights."

What are perceived as Righthaven's failings can be put into two categories: a disregard for the notion of fair use and its own lack of standing [lack of a right to file suit].

Fair use is the legal doctrine that holds that people should be permitted to make use of copyrighted material so long as they limit themselves to using only what is necessary to their message. Even copyright holders believe that this kind of sampling adds to the progress of culture or our understanding of society without harming the market for their work.

Indeed, Righthaven seemed to have been caught off guard when judges wouldn't fault bloggers for reposting photographs or quoting articles. In one of the most famous Righthaven cases, a federal judge found that Vietnam veteran Wayne Hoehn, who had posted all 19 paragraphs of a *Las Vegas Review-Journal* editorial, was within his fair use right to do so.

The issue is one of the main reasons why Randazza decided to take on the company. "It irritated me that the company filed all those cases without any regard to fair use," he says.

No Legal Standing to Sue

Righthaven's inability to anticipate and prevail on these fair use challenges has alarmed some trade groups in the content industry, including the RIAA and the Association of American Publishers, which filed an amicus brief last December at the 9th U.S. Circuit Court of Appeals at San Francisco in the Hoehn case. They argued that Righthaven lacked standing to pursue its copyright claims and shouldn't be allowed to usher in "sweeping fair use pronouncements" that would imperil real copyright owners.

That leads to Righthaven's second failing, which doesn't get quite so under the skin of its critics but is equally significant.

The idea that Righthaven lacked standing derives from successful challenges at the district court level to the way it was assigned copyrights by its media partners in the first place. One judge ruled that only plaintiffs who have actual control over copyrights can sue. Righthaven was merely given the right to sue in its "strategic alliance agreement" with Stephens Media, and the judge said that wasn't enough.

No topic arouses more anger from Gibson than this particular decision. He thinks it was a flawed one, emanating from a judge who was influenced by "personally vicious, unfounded, disreputable attacks" on Righthaven.

Critics like Dunlap aren't so sure. "If Righthaven had filed [its cases] in the name of the rights-holder like Stephens Media, then I don't think their cases would have been dismissed," he says. "I'm not sure why they didn't."

Righthaven's Motives a Mystery

Gibson could have easily represented Stephens Media as its outside counsel. Instead, he chose to step outside the lawyer's typical role and create a shell company whose sole purpose was to sue. Why?

Righthaven observers have all sorts of theories on this. Some believe Righthaven's raison d'être was greed, plain and simple. As lawyer-executives of such a company, they could grab a larger share of the potential settlements and judgments than they could as mere litigators. Others believe the media companies that held the copyrights wished to create a "firewall" between their operations and any potential adverse judgments and negative PR from the litigation campaign.

Gibson wouldn't speak to this mystery directly, perhaps because it's likely a subject of the probe by the State Bar of Nevada, which confirmed in January that it was investigating Gibson and two other Righthaven lawyers without giving any details. . . .

How about you, dear reader? When you have your Google moment and see something out there on the Web that seems to be stolen from you, what should happen? Is there an ethical way to handle the situation that's both financially reasonable and sure to be effective? Or must you acknowledge that control is out of your hands these days and there's really no recourse?

Tough questions, surely. Don't sue me for asking.

> *"The recording industry sees no coincidence in the fact that file-sharing has exploded during the same period that the market for CDs has withered."*

Music Sales Are Hurt by Copyright Infringement

Steven Seidenberg

Steven Seidenberg is a lawyer and writer who regularly contributes to ABA Journal. *In the following viewpoint, Seidenberg discusses the loss of revenue through depressed album sales that the recording industry experienced in the early twenty-first century as file sharing grew in popularity. The recording industry initially fought back through litigation, reports Seidenberg, but at the expense of its public image as the industry increasingly filed suit against individual users rather than companies. Seidenberg addresses research that shows the music industry is not suffering as much as it claims because the lost album revenue is being made up in complementary sales and the creation of new works is actually on the rise. Some pioneering minds are pursuing new approaches to music delivery, writes Seidenberg, taking advantage of Internet technology in the form of streaming licensed content.*

Steven Seindenberg, "The Record Business Blues," *ABA Journal*, vol. 96, no. 6, June 2010. Reprinted with permission from the ABA Journal. Copyright 2013, ABA Journal. All rights reserved. License #36935.

As you read, consider the following questions:

1. How much value was lost in the CD market between 2000 and 2008, according to Seidenberg?

2. According to the author, how many people have recording companies sued since 1999?

3. According to Seidenberg, what self-governing island is proposing a monthly tariff of its constituents in exchange for unlimited downloadable music?

Recession or no, the music industry has been hitting a high note lately. Reports indicate that, on average, revenues are on the rise for musical artists. Income from concerts and ancillary merchandise (such as souvenir T-shirts) has become a key revenue for most performers. New vehicles for delivering music in innovative and exciting ways are being introduced regularly. And consumers are getting more music at lower prices.

But sales of recorded music have hit a sour note. In 2000, manufacturers shipped 942.5 million music CDs with a retail value of $13.2 billion to sales outlets in the United States alone, according to the Recording Industry Association of America. By 2008, those numbers had dropped to 384.7 million CDs shipped with a retail value of $5.5 billion—a plunge in dollar value of 58 percent in only eight years. (Ironically, the only segment of the physical recordings market to grow between 2000 and 2008 was vinyl LP records, thought at one point to be headed for extinction.)

Many in the recording industry say the villain in this opera is file-sharing, which allows computer files to move back and forth freely among networks of users on the Internet. The recording industry sees no coincidence in the fact that file-sharing has exploded during the same period that the market for CDs has withered.

Piracy Is a Drain on the Economy

In the industry's view, the problem is that file-sharing is both enormously popular and almost always illegal.

In 2008, for example, 40 billion music downloads—95 percent of the total worldwide—were infringing, according to the International Federation of the Phonographic Industry.

Though the RIAA [Recording Industry Association of America] says the music industry has fully embraced the Internet as a major channel for distribution to consumers, the group has called on the Federal Communications Commission to endorse efforts to curb illegal downloads of copyrighted works.

"The full potential of those licensed digital distribution models [is] undermined by a glut of illegal file-sharing, which has inflicted enormous damage on the creative industries generally," the group said in a press release in January [2010].

Illegal file-sharing also has wider economic implications, said the RIAA, citing a 2007 report by the Institute for Policy Innovation in Lewisville, Texas. That report, titled *The True Cost of Copyright Industry Piracy to the U.S. Economy*, estimates that in 2005 at least $25.6 billion in potential revenue was lost to piracy in sound recordings, motion pictures, business software and entertainment software video games. The report claims that copyright piracy costs the U.S. economy more than 373,000 jobs annually in related fields and industries, and also results in more than $2.6 billion in lost tax revenue for local, state and federal governments every year.

"We need to get file-sharing to a level that is manageable, that allows the music industry to flourish," says Steven M. Marks, executive vice president and general counsel at the RIAA.

Winning Battles, Losing the War

The recording industry has lots of experience battling file-sharing. Since 1999, recording companies have sued some 35,000 individuals, as well as Napster, Grokster, LimeWire and

© Mike Baldwin/www.CartoonStock.com.

other companies that were making and distributing file-sharing software. Recording companies won several landmark court rulings, drove file-sharing companies out of business or into new lines of work, and collected settlements from tens of thousands of people for illegally sharing files.

But even after winning so many legal battles, the recording industry still appears to be losing the war.

"Every time the courts came out with a decision, people came out with another way to circumvent it," says Jeffrey E. Jacobson, a founding member of Jacobson & Colfin in New

York City who chairs the Broadcasting, Sound Recordings and Performance Artists Committee in the ABA [American Bar Association] Section of Intellectual Property Law.

In 2001, for instance, the industry won a legal victory that effectively killed the wildly popular Napster file-sharing service only two years after it went into operation. The San Francisco–based 9th U.S. Circuit Court of Appeals ruled in *A&M Records Inc. v. Napster Inc.* that because Napster maintained a central index of all shared files, the company knew its users were sharing copyrighted materials and could be held liable for contributory copyright infringement. The court also held that because Napster failed to take reasonable steps to police its system—and profited from file-sharing that infringed on copyrights—the company could be held liable for vicarious infringement as well.

Peer-to-Peer Software

Napster went out of business, but it was quickly replaced by Kazaa, eDonkey, BearShare, LimeWire and other companies that created and supplied decentralized file-sharing software. Users connected directly with one another, and the companies supplying this peer-to-peer, or P2P, software could not monitor or control what files users were sharing. Thus there was no infringement, whether vicarious or contributory, under the Napster standard.

A few years later, the recording industry won another landmark legal victory—this time against the P2P companies—when the U.S. Supreme Court recognized a new type of copyright claim in *MGM Studios Inc. v. Grokster Ltd.* The court ruled that P2P companies could be held liable for "inducing" copyright infringement if they marketed their software as a tool for uploading and downloading files that infringed on copyrights.

After Grokster, all the P2P companies save one admitted defeat and settled with the recording companies. (LimeWire is still battling in the courts.)

Going After Individuals, Too

But the recording companies did not limit their copyright suits to makers and distributors of file-sharing software. Starting in 2003, the labels began suing thousands of individuals who allegedly downloaded and shared copyrighted songs without authorization. Initially, this widely publicized litigation campaign drove down the frequency of file-sharing. But within months the number of file-sharers surpassed pre-lawsuit levels and kept climbing.

The odds were one-sided. The recording industry eventually filed thousands of suits, but there were millions of file-sharers. "People thought they weren't going to get caught," Jacobson says.

In late 2008, the recording companies abruptly ended their litigation campaign, announcing that they would no longer sue file-sharers for copyright infringement except in egregious circumstances.

Critics of the recording industry say its litigation campaign was bound to fail, and was a public relations disaster to boot. The industry claims, however, that the campaign was a qualified hit that raised public awareness about the illegal nature of unauthorized copying and slowed the growth of file-sharing enough to give the industry a chance to establish legal online music distribution channels.

"Litigation was a good deterrence strategy, but we thought it better to find a way that scaled more naturally," Marks says. . . .

Doubts About File-Sharing's Harm

Some researchers express doubts about the recording industry's long-standing assertion that file-sharing is killing the market for CDs and similar products in a way that will stifle the entire music field.

"There is no doubt that trade groups vastly exaggerate the impact of file-sharing on industry profitability when they treat every pirated copy as a lost sale," states "File-Sharing and Copyright," a paper issued in January by Felix Oberholzer-Gee, a professor at Harvard Business School in Cambridge, Mass., and Koleman S. Strumpf, a professor at the University of Kansas School of Business in Lawrence. "At a price close to zero, many consumers will download music and movies that they would not have bought at current prices."

Oberholzer-Gee and Strumpf say the empirical evidence of the effect of file-sharing on sales of recorded music products is mixed, and they note that many studies conclude that music piracy accounts for no more than one-fifth of the recent decline in recording sales. Moreover, the authors assert, file-sharing hasn't hurt the music industry overall: "While file-sharing disrupted some traditional business models in the creative industries, foremost in music, in our reading of the evidence there is little to suggest that the new technology has discouraged artistic production."

Indeed, Oberholzer-Gee and Strumpf indicate that despite the explosion in file-sharing over the past decade the production of new artistic works is on the rise. "The publication of new books rose by 66 percent over the 2002–07 period," wrote Oberholzer-Gee and Strumpf in their paper. "Since 2000, the annual release of new music albums has more than doubled, and worldwide feature film production is up by more than 30 percent since 2003."

The Music Industry Is Thriving

Other experts also point to what appears to be a thriving music industry despite the recent plunge in CD sales. In addition to strong revenue from concerts and souvenir sales, television and movies are paying well for songs, scores and musical performances. Lucrative new markets for music have opened up, including ringtones, ringbacks and electronic games (see Guitar Hero). Innovative companies like Pandora, Lala, Mog and Spotify are providing customers with new ways to get music online and over their cellphones. Many experts see this as the industry's future, with customers paying a fee for unlimited access to music rather than purchasing individual songs or albums.

"The large recording companies are struggling to find a new business model that is anywhere near as profitable as the old one used to be. Other parts of the music industry are doing very well," says Oberholzer-Gee.

The debate over how to respond to file-sharing of music and the products of other creative efforts also raises questions about the true purpose of copyright law.

The RIAA's Marks says the principle of copyright is simple. "It is a property right," he says. "You spend time creating something or investing in it, you should have the law grant you enough rights that your creative or financial investment is protected."

The Purpose of Copyright Law

There is, however, another view about the purpose of copyright law. Article I, section 8 of the U.S. Constitution grants Congress the power to establish copyright protections for authors and inventors to "promote the progress of science and useful arts."

To achieve that goal, copyright law creates "a system to 'incentivize' creators and their backers so they can be rewarded for the fruits of their labors so they can continue to create new works," [Beverly Hills entertainment lawyer Fred] Goldring says.

If the ultimate goal is to promote the creation of new works, then perhaps it isn't really necessary to take stronger legal actions against illegal file-sharing because the evidence does not suggest that it is hindering the creation of new works by musicians. That is, at least, the contention of Oberholzer-

Gee and Strumpf. They note in their paper that, despite the growth of illegal file-sharing, more music than ever is being created and made available to the public. "This makes it difficult to argue that weaker copyright protection has had a negative impact on artists' incentives to be creative," their paper states.

Musicians Do Not Play Just for Money

The reasons for the surge in musical output aren't entirely clear to Oberholzer-Gee, Strumpf and other researchers. They suggest that part of the answer is that making music isn't just about making money. For a lucky few music can be highly lucrative, but most musicians can't even afford to make it their full-time job.

"Given these poor prospects, why are there so many musicians?" ask Oberholzer-Gee and Strumpf in their paper. "One explanation is that musicians enjoy their profession. Under this view, musicians take pleasure from creating and performing music, as well as aspects of the lifestyle such as flexible hours and the lack of an immediate boss. If this theory is correct, the economic impact of file-sharing is not likely to have a major impact on music creation."

Not only is more music available to the public, but it has become more affordable in the era of file-sharing, which may suggest another important lesson about the real purposes of copyright law.

"For the past 200 years, we have been continually strengthening copyright protections," Oberholzer-Gee says. "We always thought we needed super-strong rights to make people create. Maybe we were wrong."

That more music at lower cost became available to the public just as copyright protections were being weakened by file-sharing suggests that the need for even stronger protection is open to question, he says.

Making File-Sharing Legal

That kind of argument won't make the charts with the music recording industry, which has shown little willingness to give up its fight to rein in illegal file-sharing. But some in the industry are showing interest in the idea of making file-sharing legal.

The idea goes like this: Impose a blanket license on copyright owners, making it legal for all their musical works to be shared online. In return, ISP [internet service provider] customers would pay a monthly licensing fee. Music rights organizations like ASCAP [American Society of Composers, Authors and Publishers] and BMI [Broadcast Music, Inc.] would collect the licensing fees and distribute royalty payments to performers and songwriters.

"If we were getting $2 or $3 monthly for each family with a broadband connection, and music royalties were distributed based on what people were listening to or downloading, that becomes significant money," says Ted Cohen, a former music company executive who is now managing partner at Tag Strategic in Los Angeles, a consulting firm for the digital entertainment industry. "That ultimately is the solution to file-sharing."

Cohen says an experiment in legal file-sharing may soon be launched by the Isle of Man, a self-governing British possession in the Irish Sea. The island's government has proposed a small monthly tariff on each customer's ISP connection, which would allow the customer to download an unlimited amount of music. A customer may opt out of the plan, but if the user is caught downloading a copyright-protected file just once, his or her Internet connection will be terminated.

Licensed Music Streams Are Common

Variations on all-you-can-hear music plans already are being offered by some innovative Internet music providers. Slacker and Pandora, for instance, offer the option of creating customized music streams that are playable on a customer's computer, iPhone or BlackBerry. Spotify and Mog both enable users to select and stream an unlimited number of tracks or albums. These plans offer consumers the ability to hear a huge selection of music for a low monthly fee instead of spending large amounts of money to amass their own collections of songs.

By making music cheap and easy to access—and by offering other consumer-friendly add-ons, such as lyrics and online music communities—these providers may be showing the way on how to put the clamps on infringing file-sharing, many experts believe.

"The best way to stamp out file-sharing is by creating better, new, licensed legal models, which make it more attractive not to pirate than to pirate," says Fred Davis, an attorney and founding partner of Code Advisors, an investment bank in New York City that focuses on technology and new media. "We're on the frontier of those new models, and that's what the future of the music industry holds."

Periodical and Internet Sources Bibliography

The following articles have been selected to supplement the diverse viewpoints presented in this chapter.

Erik Kain   "Does Piracy Cause Economic Harm? How to Think About Economic Frontiers," *Forbes*, January 15, 2012.

Christopher Kellen   "The Economics of DRM, Ebooks and Piracy," Eye of the Storm, May 31, 2012. www.christopherkellen.com.

David Lowery   "Letter to Emily White at NPR *All Things Considered*," *The Trichordist* (blog), June 18, 2012. http://thetrichordist.com.

Eduardo Porter   "The Perpetual War: Pirates and Creators," *New York Times*, February 4, 2012.

Bill Rosenblatt   "Yes, Piracy Does Cause Economic Harm," *Copyright and Technology*, January 27, 2013. www.copyrightandtechnology.com.

David Scheuermann   "Manufacturing Discontent: Flexible Copyright Laws Are Good for Economy, Innovation," *LSU Daily Reveille*, September 26, 2012. www.lsureveille.com.

Lamar Smith   "Why We Need a Law Against Online Piracy," CNN.com, January 20, 2012. www.cnn.com.

Michael D. Smith and Rahul Telang   "Assessing the Academic Literature Regarding the Impact of Media Piracy on Sales," Social Science Research Network, August 2012. http://papers.ssrn.com.

Beverly Storrs   "Piracy Is Stealing and Affecting Music Industry," *Digital Universe*, February 21, 2012. http://universe.byu.edu.

Rob Reid   "The Numbers Behind the Copyright Math," *TED Blog*, March 20, 2012. http://blog.ted.com.

CHAPTER 3

Is Copyright Law Effective?

Chapter Preface

The stated purpose of the US Copyright Act is to promote the arts and sciences by creating incentives for people to create and innovate. The increasing concern by copyright holders with litigation and profit loses sight of this primary aim, but as many have argued, litigation is necessary to protect copyrighted work, especially in the digital age when people can turn quite casually to infringement to get what they want.

The US Register of Copyrights, Maria Pallante, told Congress in March 2013 that a broad overhaul of copyright law was necessary, including digital fair use, orphan works, royalties, and length of copyright. Digital media have transformed copyright industries and the economy overall by significantly changing how companies reproduce products and how people exchange money for goods and services. If copyright reform is inevitable, the question then becomes whether reform should move forward or backward.

The Copyright Act of 1978 extended protection for corporations to seventy-five years and for individuals to life of the creator plus fifty years. The controversial Copyright Term Extension Act of 1998 amended this protection to include an additional twenty years for both corporations and individuals. If we were to "move backward," returning to the original intent of the 1978 law, more content would be in the public domain, providing greater opportunity for derivative works and other innovative applications (for example, a stage adaptation of a book or film).

For the sake of argument, "moving forward" would probably extend protection further and would codify case law concerning fair use, first sale doctrine, and anti-circumnavigation (getting around rights protections). Corporations, such as the Hollywood film industry, and top-earning performers who feel their income is impacted by infringement, support a strengthening and lengthening of copyright protection. By contrast, creators who are emerging in their field—such as self-published science fiction author Hugh Howey—are often helped by infringement because the resulting increases in exposure and traffic boosts their income and popularity. Howey wrote a post on his blog in May 2012, "Me and the Pirates Are Tight," in which he explained his decision to not use digital rights management (DRM) on his books: "I wanted to reward the buyer rather than worry about the pirate." Howey even claims that people who have illegally downloaded his books have later sent him money because they enjoyed them so much.

The debate over whether a few self-made authors and performers equate to an economically sound new model of doing business in the copyright industries and whether longer and more involved copyright protections serve the original purpose of the Copyright Act "to promote the Progress of Science and useful Arts" are just some of the questions relating to the effectiveness of copyright law debated by the authors of the viewpoints in the following chapter.

| "Copyright owners generally will be advantaged [by court rulings on the DMCA] in their efforts to use technical means to block unauthorized access to their works."

The Digital Millennium Copyright Act Protects Against Copyright Infringement

Jeffrey D. Neuburger

Jeffrey D. Neuburger is a lawyer specializing in technology and data security. In the following viewpoint, Neuburger reviews the copyright lawsuit brought against MDY Industries by Blizzard Entertainment for MDY's creation and application of bot software, called Glider, to accelerate players through the lower, easy levels of the popular online game World of Warcraft, which is distributed by Blizzard. Although Blizzard created an anti-bot software called Warden to prevent players from using Glider, Neuburger explains, MDY engineered Glider to work around Warden. This circumnavigation lay at the heart of the case, and the Ninth Circuit Court of Appeals found in 2010, Neuburger

Jeffrey D. Neuburger, "The Ninth Circuit's World of Warcraft Decision: The Copyright and DMCA Issues," *Intellectual Property and Technology Law Journal*, April 2011. Copyright © 2011 by Jeffrey D. Neuburger. All rights reserved. Reproduced permission.

reports, that MDY was liable for contributory copyright infringement under the DMCA [Digital Millennium Copyright Act] but was not responsible for contract interference.

As you read, consider the following questions:

1. According to Neuburger, how much gross revenue did Glider's creator, Michael Donnelly, earn after only a few years of selling Glider licenses?

2. According to the author, what are some examples of evidence that MDY submitted to support its argument that Glider has positive effects on people's lives?

3. What did the Ninth Circuit Court of Appeals decide after examining Warden's ability to prevent copying, according to the author?

Playing World of Warcraft, the world's most popular massively multiplayer online role-playing game (MMORPG), can be, well, a drag. As the parents, teachers, and spouses of gamers know all too well, playing through the 70 or more levels of the game in order to amass desired virtual currency, weapons, and armor can be extremely time-consuming so some gamers have resorted to the use of bots (automated game-playing software robots) to make their way more quickly from the more tedious early levels of the game to the more interesting upper levels. Michael Donnelly developed WoW bot software (Glider) for his own use, and it worked so well that he decided to sell it to other gamers. And that worked well, too. In a few years, Donnelly (incorporated as MDY Industries) had gross revenues of $3.5 million from sales of Glider licenses.

The Distributor Strikes Back

For Blizzard Entertainment, the distributor of WoW software and the operator of the servers that enable online game play, bots are, well, a drag. Other gamers complain that they constitute cheating, and Blizzard potentially loses revenue when gamers finish the game sooner rather than later, so Blizzard added a provision to the WoW terms of use prohibiting the use of bots and similar third-party software. WoW also deployed a software solution, WoW Warden, that checks gamers' computers for prohibited software and prevents their access to the server if it is present. Warden works only so-so at blocking Glider-using players, though, and it costs a lot of money to deploy and maintain.

Blizzard also sent its lawyers to Donnelly's home to personally demand that he cease selling the Glider program. (Whether he called them Worgen and tried to repel them with his Corpse-Impaling Spike [a World of Warcraft tactic] is not part of the record.) Donnelly subsequently filed an action seeking a declaratory judgment that his sale of the Glider program did not infringe Blizzard's copyrights, and Blizzard responded with counterclaims under copyright law, the Digital Millennium Copyright Act (DMCA), and state law.

Game on.

Copyright Issues the Case Raises

The dispute between MDY and Blizzard raises interesting issues under copyright law and the DMCA, issues on which the US Court of Appeals for the Ninth Circuit ruled recently in *MDY Industries, LLC v. Blizzard Entertainment, Inc.* The ruling was largely, although not completely, favorable to Blizzard, but either way it is an important ruling for content and software licensors that seek to control the use of their copyrighted works.

The case was argued on the same day, and before the same panel, as *Vernor v. Autodesk*, in which the court defined the circumstances under which a purchaser of software is a licensee, not an owner of a copy, for purposes of the copyright first-sale doctrine. That ruling comes into play in *MDY v. Blizzard*; in a slam-dunk application of *Vernor*, the court found that the WoW gamers are licensees, not owners, of a copy of their WoW software. In this article, however, we'll look at a different issue addressed by the court: whether gamers who use the Glider software in violation of Blizzard's ToU [terms of use] are infringing Blizzard's copyrights. That was an essential question because, if the gamers were not directly infringing Blizzard's copyrights, then MDY and Donnelly could not be held secondarily liable for copyright infringement for selling them the means by which to infringe—the Glider software.

ToU Violators Are Not Infringing

MDY and Donnelly conceded that the use of Glider by WoW players violated the ToU, but they argued that Glider users were not infringers. Rather, they argued, the ToU's prohibition against the use of bots is a covenant, not a license condition, and a breach of a covenant gives rise only to a claim for breach of contract, not copyright infringement.

The appeals court agreed with MDY and Donnelly, holding that "a potential for infringement exists only where the licensee's action (1) exceeds the license's scope (2) in a manner that implicates one of the licensor's exclusive statutory rights." The use of Glider did not implicate any of Blizzard's exclusive rights, the court found, because its use did not, for example, either alter or copy the WoW software. For there to be infringement, the court concluded, there must be a nexus between the license condition and an exclusive right of copyright:

> Were we to hold otherwise, Blizzard—or any software copyright holder—could designate any disfavored conduct during software use as copyright infringement, by purporting to condition the license on the player's abstention from the disfavored conduct. The rationale would be that because the conduct occurs while the player's computer is copying the software code into RAM [the computer's memory] in order

A New Penalty for DMCA Infringers

Has someone filed a large number of DMCA "takedown" requests against your Site? If so, look out. There's a new penalty that may cause you to rank lower in Google's search results. It joins other penalties (also called "filters" or "updates") such as "Panda" and "Penguin." We're dubbing this one the "Pirate Update" as it's aimed at copyright piracy. . . .

Why not do this before? Personally, my own feeling is that Google—now a content distribution company that really wants partnerships—has finally decided it needs to deal with the embarrassing situation of pirated content showing up in its results. . . . For its part, Google says the change is only now happening because it finally has the data it needs.

Danny Sullivan, Search Engine Land,
August 10, 2012. http://searchengineland.com.

for it to run, the violation is copyright infringement. This would allow software copyright owners far greater rights than Congress has generally conferred on copyright owners.

So, the appeals court overruled the district court's grant of summary judgment in favor of Blizzard on its claims of contributory and vicarious copyright infringement.

The Case Raises a New Issue

Interestingly, in a footnote, the court raised a point not at issue in the case: whether the continued use of a licensed work without making required payments constitutes copyright infringement. The court commented that such a licensee:

arguably may commit copyright infringement by continuing to use the licensed work while failing to make required payments, even though a failure to make payments otherwise lacks a nexus to the licensor's exclusive statutory rights. We view payment as sui generis [unique], however, because of the distinct nexus between payment and all commercial copyright licenses, not just those concerning software.

Perhaps all commercial copyright licenses do not have a nexus with payment; consider the case of open source licenses. In the 2008 Federal Circuit decision *Jacobsen v. Katzer*, the Federal Circuit rejected the argument that an open source license was not enforceable under copyright law because the licensed software was distributed free of charge. Further, the court held that a provision in an open source license requiring the inclusion of author, license, and copyright information if the software was modified and redistributed was a condition enforceable under copyright law, not a mere covenant. The appeals court relied upon language in the license identifying the attribution requirements as a condition and a general policy favoring the enforcement of open source licenses. The result in *Jacobsen v. Katzer*, if not its reasoning, is probably consistent with *MDY v. Blizzard*, as the rights that were being conditioned were the right to modify and distribute the software, rights that are unquestionably exclusive rights of the copyright holder.

Blizzard Related Claim vs. MDY

Back to *MDY v. Blizzard*. Although MDY and Donnelly escaped liability for copyright infringement, the court's ruling had the effect of boosting Blizzard's related state law claim that MDY tortiously [noncriminally but still illegally] interfered with its contracts with WoW licensees because, the court ruled, the Copyright Act does not preempt a breach-of-contract claim that is not equivalent to any exclusive right of copyright. But while the district court had granted summary judgment against MDY and Donnelly on the breach-of-contract claims, the Ninth Circuit reversed the entry of judgment, finding that there were outstanding material issues of fact on one of the elements of such a claim: whether MDY's actions were "improper" under the seven-factor test of Restatement (Second) of Torts [section] 767. Accordingly, among the issues to be considered on remand are "the social interests in protecting MDY's freedom of action and Blizzard's contractual interests," about which the court commented:

> Blizzard argues that it seeks to provide its millions of WoW players with a particular role-playing game experience that excludes bots. . . . In contrast, MDY argues that Glider is an innovative, profitable software program that has positively affected its users' lives by advancing them to WoW's more interesting levels. MDY has introduced evidence that Glider allows players with limited motor skills to continue to play WoW, improves some users' romantic relationships by reducing the time that they spend playing WoW, and allows users who work long hours to play WoW.

Glider has a positive effect on gamers' romantic lives? That should be an interesting trial on the merits.

Do Bots Violate the DMCA?

As noted earlier, Blizzard Entertainment, distributor of the World of Warcraft game software and the operator of the servers that enable online game play, sought to block the use of automated game playing software by deploying anti-bot software, WoW Warden. But MDY Industries, the distributor of the Glider bot software, countered that move by reengineering Glider to evade detection by Warden and enable users to continue to access WoW's servers while using the bot. This feature of Glider is the basis for Blizzard's claims that MDY violated the provisions of the DMCA that prohibit trafficking in software and other devices that enable circumvention of copyright protection technologies.

In *MDY Industries, LLC v. Blizzard Entertainment, Inc.*, the Ninth Circuit commenced its analysis of the DMCA issues by parsing the complex interconnection between the two parallel prohibitions in the anticircumvention provisions: the prohibition in [section] 1201(a) against the circumvention of a technological measure that "effectively controls access to a work protected under this title," i.e., a copyrighted work, and the prohibition in [section] 1201(b) against the circumvention of a technological measure that "effectively protects a right of a copyright owner." It is important to note the difference between the two sections: [section] 1201(a) protects measures that limit access to a copyrighted work, while [section] 1201(b) protects measures that protect a right of a copyright owner.

The appeals court concluded that a copyright owner's rights in [section] 1201(a) are, in effect, broader than a copyright owner's rights under [section] 1201(b) because "preventing 'access' to a protected work in itself has not been a right of a copyright owner arising from the Copyright Act." Thus, the court said, "we read this term as extending a new form of protection, i.e., the right to prevent circumvention of access controls, broadly to . . . copyrighted works."

Legal Precedents Support Copyright Owners

The court explicitly rejected the argument that [section] 1201(a) should be more narrowly construed and should be applied only when there is a nexus between the access sought to be prevented and a copyright owner's rights under the Copyright Act. Such a nexus was required by the Federal Circuit in its 2004 decision in *Chamberlain Group, Inc. v. Skylink Technologies, Inc.*, where a manufacturer of garage door openers that contained copyrighted firmware unsuccessfully sought to use the anticircumvention provisions to bar the use of third-party replacement controls that required access to the firmware in order to activate the opener.

As the Ninth Circuit in *MDY v. Blizzard* acknowledged, in *Chamberlain*, the Federal Circuit "feared that Section 1201(a) would allow companies to leverage their sales into aftermarket monopolies, in tension with antitrust law and the doctrine of copyright misuse." The Ninth Circuit concluded that the policy concerns that the Federal Circuit relied on in *Chamberlain* were not present in *MDY v. Blizzard* and that the potential interplay between antitrust law and [section] 1201(a) could be reserved for future cases. In any event, the Ninth Circuit concluded, those policy concerns should not prevail over the plain language of the statute and the legislative history that it carefully and extensively examined.

The Ninth Circuit also left for future consideration the issue of whether fair use is a defense to a prima facie [apparent] violation of [section] 1201, because MDY did not claim that the use of Glider was protected by the doctrine of fair use.

Determining What Warden Does

The next question the court tackled was whether Blizzard's Warden software either "effectively controls access" to a copyrighted work or "effectively protects a right of a copyright owner," and that requires understanding of how the WoW software is structured and how the Warden program works.

The WoW software consists of two components: a game client that is installed on the user's computer and game elements that are available only when the user is connected to the WoW servers. The court divided the protectable elements of the WoW software into three buckets: (1) the literal elements of the software (the game client's software code that resides on the user's computer), (2) the individual non-literal elements (individual components, such as recorded sounds and images that are stored locally and called up by the game client software in the course of play), and (3) the game's dynamic, non-literal elements, the "real-time experience of traveling through different worlds, hearing their sounds, viewing their structures, encountering their inhabitants and monsters, and encountering other players." This last element is available only when the user is connected to the WoW servers.

The Warden program has two functions. First, it scans the random access memory (RAM) of a user's computer before the user connects to WoW's online game servers to see if a bot is running, and second, it periodically scans the user's RAM to look for patterns of code that it has identified as belonging to bots and other cheating software. When it detects a bot before the user has connected to a game server, it prevents the user from logging on to the server, and if it detects a bot during play, it boots the player from the server.

The Ruling Is a Mixed Bag

Given the manner in which Warden functions, the court concluded that it does not prevent access to either the of the WoW elements that are stored locally on a user's computer, because those elements are accessible to a user despite the presence of Warden. But Warden does prevent access to WoW's dynamic, non-literal elements that are accessible only when connected to WoW's servers. Accordingly, the appeals court found that Warden is a technological measure that "effectively controls access" to a copyrighted work and that MDY had engaged in trafficking in a technology, Glider, that circumvents that control in violation of [section] 1201(a)(2).

MDY was not found to violate [section] 1201(b). Blizzard argued that Warden effectively protected its right against unauthorized copying in various respects, but the court disagreed. Because WoW gamers are authorized to load the game code into RAM, a user of Glider who continues to load code into RAM despite Warden's efforts to interrupt that process is not infringing, the court found. Because WoW players using Glider are able to log on to the game server and access the dynamic non-literal elements of the game despite Warden's efforts, Warden doesn't "effectively" protect against copying.

For Blizzard, although the ruling is a mixed bag, the result is certainly not a total loss. At the end of the day its [section] 1201(a) trafficking claim survived with respect to protecting WoW's dynamic, nonliteral elements from copying and is likely to be a sufficient basis for the district court to reissue an injunction and award of damages. Although summary judgment on Blizzard's tortious interference claim was vacated, it may still press that claim on remand.

DMCA Provides New Possibilities

For users of software and other copyrighted works, the aspects of the ruling dealing with the issue of contract covenants and copyright conditions narrows the circumstances under which they might be found to be copyright infringers, should they violate a provision in a terms-of-use or similar document. Accordingly, service providers may be limited in using the stern remedies of the Copyright Act to control unwanted access to their systems, at least in the Ninth Circuit. In that respect, see, for example, the 2009 decision by the US District Court for the Northern District of California in *Facebook, Inc. v. Power Ventures, Inc.*

For device manufacturers that, like the garage door opener manufacturer in *Chamberlain*, wish to use the DMCA anticircumvention provisions for competitive advantage, the ruling may present new possibilities for structuring their products. And of course, copyright owners generally will be advantaged in their efforts to use technical means to block unauthorized access to their works.

For the DMCA itself, the ruling in *MDY v. Blizzard* sets up a circuit split on the construction of the anticircumvention provisions and presents the possibility of US Supreme Court review or possibly a reexamination of the ruling by the Ninth Circuit en banc [with all the judges ruling], a remedy that either or both sides in the case might well seek.

"*Years of experience with the ... DMCA demonstrate that the statute reaches too far, chilling a wide variety of legitimate activities.*"

The Digital Millennium Copyright Act Jeopardizes Fair Use

Fred von Lohmann

Fred von Lohmann is a lawyer who specializes in copyright law. He was senior staff attorney at the Electronic Frontier Foundation before being hired onto Google's legal team in 2010. In the following viewpoint, Von Lohmann examines the negative impact of the Digital Millennium Copyright Act (DMCA) on fair uses of copyrighted material. For example, Von Lohmann explains, after the failed application of DRM-restricted files, customers are left with no legitimate recourse for moving those files to new devices because companies no longer support the necessary software and access. The DMCA anti-circumnavigation law blocks numerous fair uses, including copying physical DVDs onto mobile devices and computers for personal and educational use, copying e-books for personal use, and time-shifting streaming media for personal use, according to the author. Von Lohmann concludes that in the modern world where everything is digital, the DMCA reaches far beyond what Congress intended.

As you read, consider the following questions:

1. According to Von Lohmann, why was the company Real-Networks forced to stop selling its RealDVD software?

2. What fair uses did the Advanced E-book Processor software permit readers to engage in, according to the author, before the software was deemed illegal and pulled from distribution?

3. Why are laws against space shifting DVDs financially convenient for movie studios, according to the author?

"Fair use" is a crucial element in American copyright law—the principle that the public is entitled, without having to ask permission, to use copyrighted works in ways that do not unduly interfere with the copyright owner's market for a work. Fair uses include personal, noncommercial uses, such as using a VCR to record a television program for later viewing. Fair use also includes activities undertaken for purposes such as criticism, comment, news reporting, teaching, scholarship or research.

The DMCA Dooms Fair Use

We are entering an era where digital content—including e-books and video—is "copy-protected" and otherwise restricted by technological means. Whether scholars, researchers, commentators and the public will continue to be able to make legitimate fair uses of these works will depend upon the availability of tools to bypass these digital locks.

The DMCA [Digital Millennia Copyright Act], however, prohibits the creation or distribution of these tools, even if they are crucial to fair use. So, as copyright owners use technology to press into the 21st century, the public will see fair uses whittled away by digital locks allegedly intended to "prevent piracy." Perhaps more importantly, future fair uses may not be developed for restricted media, because courts will never have the opportunity to rule on them. Fair users will be found liable for "picking the lock" and thereby violating the DMCA, whatever the merits of their fair use defense.

Copyright owners argue that these tools, in the hands of copyright infringers, can result in "Internet piracy." But banning the tools that enable fair use will punish the innocent along with infringers. Photocopiers, VCRs, and CD-R burners can also be misused, but no one would suggest that the public give them up simply because they might be used by others to break the law.

Although the Copyright Office is empowered to grant limited DMCA exemptions in a triennial rulemaking, it has repeatedly refused to grant exemptions for consumer fair uses.

Digital Rights Management Harms Fair Use

"Copy-protected" CDs and digital rights management (DRM) for online music illustrate the collision between fair use and the DMCA in the music world. Although major labels abandoned CD copy-protection after the Sony-BMG "rootkit" scandal in late-2005, more than 15 million copy-protected CDs were distributed.

Such CD copy-protection technologies interfered with the fair use expectations of music fans by inhibiting the transfer of music from CD to iPods or other MP3 players—despite the fact that making an MP3 copy of a CD for personal use qualifies as a fair use. Other fair uses impaired by copy-protection technologies include making "mix CDs" or making copies of a CD for the office or car. Unfortunately, companies that distribute tools to "repair" these dysfunctional CDs, restoring to consumers their fair use privileges, run the risk of lawsuits under the DMCA's ban on circumvention tools and technologies.

Until 2007, authorized digital music download services also utilized DRM systems that frustrated fair use expectations, and technical restrictions remain common for subscription services. And even after music download retailers like iTunes and Amazon.com gave up DRM, consumers who had purchased DRM-restricted files in the past continued to have difficulties as vendors like Walmart shut down the "authentication servers" without which DRM-restricted files could not be transferred to new computers. In other words, rather than prevent piracy, these DRM restrictions have hurt legitimate customers long after they purchased the songs.

Legitimate DVD Copying Is Blocked

There are many legitimate reasons to copy DVDs. Once the video is on the PC, for example, lots of fair uses become possible—for example, video creators can remix movie clips into original YouTube videos, frequent travelers can load the movie into their laptops, and DVD owners can skip the otherwise "unskippable" commercials that preface certain films. Without the tools necessary to copy DVDs, however, these fair uses become more difficult or impossible.

DMCA lawsuits targeting makers of DVD copying tools have hampered these and other fair uses of DVDs. In the *Universal v. Reimerdes* case, . . . the court held that the DMCA bans DeCSS, the first of many widely available free tools for decrypting and copying DVDs. In another case, federal courts ordered 321 Studios' DVD X Copy product taken off the shelves for violating the DMCA. Major movie studios also used the DMCA to sue Tritton Technologies, the manufacturer of DVD CopyWare, and three website distributors of similar software.

In October 2008, RealNetworks was forced to stop sales of its RealDVD software, designed to allow users to copy a DVD and store it on their hard drive. This format-shifting by RealDVD would have enabled DVD owners to create backups, organize a movie collection digitally, and watch a DVD at any time without being tied to a physical disc. Nor did RealDVD represent a "piracy" threat: RealDVD preserved the DVD's CSS copy-protection system and added numerous additional security measures. RealNetworks also took a license from the DVD Copy Control Association to perform the necessary DVD decryption. Nevertheless, a federal court ruled in August 2009 that, even if the uses enabled by RealDVD were lawful fair uses, the DMCA forbids the distribution of tools like RealDVD.

Fair Use Is Blocked by the DMCA

In light of these rulings, movie fans, film scholars, movie critics, educators, librarians, video remixers, and public interest groups have been forced to ask the Copyright Office repeatedly for DMCA exemptions to allow the decryption of DVDs in order to enable noninfringing uses. For example, exemptions have been sought to allow movie critics to post movie clips, DVD owners to skip "unskippable" previews and commercials, and legitimate purchasers to bypass "region coding" restrictions on their DVD players. Every DVD-related request was denied in both the 2000 and 2003 triennial rulemakings. In 2006, a narrow DMCA exemption was granted to allow film professors to create compilations of motion pictures for educational use in the classroom.

In 2009, educators renewed their request for an exemption that would allow film professors, media studies educators, and students to use short clips taken from DVDs for educational purposes. EFF [Electronic Frontier Foundation] and the Organization for Transformative Works also applied for an exemption to allow remixers to extract clips from DVDs to create noncommercial remix videos. While the motion picture industry endorsed a renewal of the narrow exemption for film professors, it opposed any expansion to permit other noninfringing uses of DVDs, going so far as to suggest that noninfringing users should camcord DVD clips from flat screen televisions. As of February 2010, the Copyright Office had not yet ruled on the 2009 exemption proposals.

Even if other narrow exemptions are granted in the future, it is worth noting that the Copyright Office is powerless to grant an exemption to the DMCA's "tools" ban. As a result, even if fair users succeed in obtaining a DMCA exemption, technology companies will remain reluctant to supply them with the necessary circumvention tools.

The DMCA Blocks Fair Use of E-books

The future of fair use for books was at issue in the criminal prosecution of Dmitry Sklyarov and Elcomsoft. Elcomsoft produced and distributed a tool called the Advanced e-Book Processor, which translates e-books from Adobe's e-book format to PDF. This translation process removed various restrictions (against copying, printing, text-to-speech processing, etc.) that publishers can impose on e-books.

The Advanced e-Book Processor allowed those who have legitimately purchased e-books to make fair uses of their e-books, uses otherwise made impossible by the restrictions of the Adobe e-book format. For instance, the program allowed people to engage in the following fair uses:

- to read the e-book on a laptop or computer other than the one on which it was first downloaded;

- to continue to access the e-book in the future, if the particular technological device for which it was purchased becomes obsolete;

- to print an e-book on paper;

- to read an e-book on an alternative operating system such as Linux (Adobe's format works only on Macs and Windows PCs);

- to have a computer read an e-book out loud using text-to-speech software, which is particularly important for visually-impaired individuals.

The DMCA Blocks Recording of Streaming Media

As more people receive audio and video content from "streaming" Internet media sources, they will want tools to preserve their settled fair use expectations, including the ability to "time-shift" programming for later listening or viewing. As a result of the DMCA, however, the digital equivalents of VCRs and cassette decks for streaming media may never arrive.

Start-up software company Streambox developed exactly such a product, known simply as the Streambox VCR, designed to time-shift streaming media. When RealNetworks discovered that the Streambox VCR could time-shift streaming RealAudio webcasts, it invoked the DMCA and obtained an injunction against the Streambox VCR product (years later, this ruling would come to haunt RealNetworks when it found itself the target of a DMCA lawsuit over its own RealDVD software).

The DMCA has also been invoked to threaten the developer of an open source, noncommercial software application known as Streamripper that records MP3 audio streams for later listening.

Challenging Typeface Tools

In January 2002, typeface vendor Agfa Monotype Corporation threatened a college student with DMCA liability for creating "Embed," a free, open source, noncommercial software program designed to manipulate TrueType fonts.

According to the student:

> I wrote Embed in 1997, after discovering that all of my fonts disallowed embedding in documents. Since my fonts are free, this was silly—but I didn't want to take the time to . . . change the flag, and then reset all of the extended font properties with a separate program. What a bore! Instead, I wrote this program to convert all of my fonts at once. The program is very simple; it just requires setting a few bits to zero. Indeed, I noticed that other fonts that were licensed for unlimited distribution also disallowed embedding. . . . So, I put this program on the web in hopes that it would help other font developers as well.

Agfa Monotype nevertheless threatened the student author with DMCA liability for distributing the program. According to Agfa, the fact that Embed can be used to allow distribution of protected fonts made it contraband under section 1201, notwithstanding the fact that the tool had many legitimate uses in the hands of hobbyist font developers.

Agfa Monotype brought similar DMCA challenges against Adobe Systems for its Acrobat 5.0's Free-Text Tool and Forms Tool, which allowed so-called "editable embedding." Agfa claimed that with Acrobat 5.0, the recipient of an electronic document could make use of embedded fonts to change the contents of a form field or free text annotation, thus "circumventing" the embedding bits of some of Agfa's TrueType Fonts.

Fortunately, in 2005, a federal court found that Adobe had not violated either section 1201(a) or section 1201(b) of the DMCA. The court noted that embedding bits do not effectively control access to a protected work and, moreover, that Acrobat 5.0 was not designed primarily to circumvent TrueType fonts.

Customers Cannot Copy Their Own DVDs

In November 2006, movie studios used the DMCA against Load-'N-Go, a small company that loaded DVDs purchased by a customer onto the customer's iPod. Load-'N-Go would take DVDs purchased by the customer, load them onto her iPod, and then return both the iPod and the original DVDs.

The movie studios claimed this service violated the DMCA because creating a duplicate copy of the movie—even for personal, fair uses—circumvents the DVD's CSS encryption. Under this theory, any individual attempting to space-shift movies from DVD to iPod or to any other digital media player is violating the DMCA. Conveniently for movie studios, this legal posture enables them to sell consumers the same movies multiple times, for multiple devices.

After some back-and-forth in the courts, the case settled in February 2007. . . .

The DMCA Is Too Far-Reaching

Years of experience with the "anti-circumvention" provisions of the DMCA demonstrate that the statute reaches too far, chilling a wide variety of legitimate activities in ways Congress did not intend. As an increasing number of copyright works are wrapped in technological protection measures, it is likely that the DMCA's anti-circumvention provisions will be applied in further unforeseen contexts, hindering the legitimate activities of innovators, researchers, the press, and the public at large.

> *"Data suggest that, once informed about the alleged content theft and its possible consequences, most Internet subscribers will quickly take steps to ensure that the theft doesn't happen again."*

The Copyright Alert System Will Prevent Copyright Infringement

Recording Industry Association of America

The Recording Industry Association of America (RIAA) is a powerful trade organization that represents US record labels and distributors. In the following viewpoint, the RIAA announces the implementation of a new voluntary system for copyright infringement notification called the Copyright Alert System. Unlike the RIAA's previous litigious approach to infringement, the Copyright Alert System works with Internet service providers (ISPs) to notify consumers when their account is being used for illegal activities, such as downloading movies or music. The RIAA is confident that most consumers are either not aware that what they are doing is illegal or that their account is being used by someone else for illegal activity. According to the RIAA, notification will result in most consumers working to stop the infringement themselves.

As you read, consider the following questions:

1. According to the RIAA, how many jobs are lost each year as a result of content theft?
2. What law was enacted to put the Copyright Alert System into effect, according to the viewpoint?
3. What internet service providers (ISPs) are collaborating on the Copyright Alert System, according to the RIAA?

Leaders from the movie, television, music and Internet service provider communities today announced a landmark agreement on a common framework for "Copyright Alerts"—a state-of-the-art system similar to credit card fraud alerts—that will educate and notify Internet subscribers when their Internet service accounts possibly are being misused for online content theft. This voluntary landmark collaboration will educate subscribers about content theft on their Internet accounts benefits consumers and copyright holders alike.

Most Content Theft Stops After Notification

Every year, content theft costs the U.S. economy more than 373,000 jobs, $16 billion in lost earnings, and $3 billion in lost federal, state and local government tax revenue.

Today [July 2011], many Internet Service Providers (ISPs) forward to subscribers notifications that they receive from content owners about alleged content theft—generally by email. Until now, however, there has been no common framework of "best practices" to effectively alert subscribers, protect copyrighted content and promote access to legal online content.

The *Copyright Alert System* is based on a consumer's "right to know" when his or her Internet account may have been used improperly to download copyrighted content. Often, subscribers—particularly parents or caregivers—are not aware that their Internet accounts are being used for online content theft. Other subscribers may be unaware that downloading copyrighted content from illicit sources is illegal and violates their ISP's Terms of Service or other published policies. Data suggest that, once informed about the alleged content theft and its possible consequences, most Internet subscribers will quickly take steps to ensure that the theft doesn't happen again.

The Copyright Alert System Will Help Subscribers Protect Their Accounts from Misuse

The new *Copyright Alert System* addresses these problems with a series of early alerts—up to six—in electronic form, notifying the subscriber that his or her account may have been misused for online content theft of film, TV shows or music. It will also put in place a system of "mitigation measures" intended to stop online content theft on those accounts that appear persistently to fail to respond to repeated Copyright Alerts. The system will also provide subscribers the opportunity for an independent review to determine whether a consumer's online activity in question is lawful or if their account was identified in error. There are no new laws or regulations established as a part of this voluntary agreement. Termination of a subscriber's account is not part of this agreement. ISPs will not provide their subscribers' names to rights' holders under this agreement.

The agreement also establishes a *Center for Copyright Information* to support implementation of the system and educate consumers about the importance of copyright.

Most Consumers Do Not Want to Commit Copyright Infringement

The parties are very grateful to Governor Andrew Cuomo for his deep involvement and personal efforts, as Attorney General of the State of New York, to bring the parties together and successfully launch the negotiations that have now led to the creation of the *Copyright Alert System.*

"This groundbreaking agreement ushers in a new day and a fresh approach to addressing the digital theft of copyrighted works," said Cary Sherman, President of the Recording Industry Association of America (RIAA). "We hope that it signals a new era in which all of us in the technology and entertainment value chain work collaboratively to make the Internet a more safe and legal experience for users. It is a significant step forward not only for the creative community, which invests in and brings great entertainment to the public, but for consumers and the legitimate online marketplace as well."

"Consumers have a right to know if their broadband account is being used for illegal online content theft, or if their own online activity infringes on copyright rules—inadvertently or otherwise—so that they can correct that activity," said James Assey, Executive Vice President of the National Cable & Telecommunications Association (NCTA), which worked in an advisory capacity with ISPs to help complete the agreement. "We are confident that, once informed that content theft is taking place on their accounts, the great majority of broadband subscribers will take steps to stop it. That's why the educational nature of this initiative is so critical."

Copyright Infringement Endangers People's Jobs

"Many people don't realize that content theft puts jobs—and future productions of films, TV shows, music, and other content—at risk," said Michael O'Leary, Executive Vice President for Government Relations at the Motion Picture Association of America, Inc. (MPAA). "Today, there are more ways to enjoy content legitimately online than ever before. This agreement will help direct consumers to legal platforms rather than illicit sites, which often funnel profits to criminals rather than the artists and technicians whose hard work makes movies, television, and music possible."

"This is a sensible approach to the problem of online-content theft and, importantly, one that respects the privacy and rights of our subscribers," said Randal S. Milch, Executive Vice President and General Counsel of Verizon. "This broad industry effort builds on existing agreements with several copyright owners to forward their notices of alleged infringement to ISP subscribers. We hope that effort—designed to notify and educate customers, not to penalize them—will set a reasonable standard for both copyright owners and ISPs to follow, while informing customers about copyright laws and encouraging them to get content from the many legal sources that exist."

Jean Prewitt, President & CEO of the Independent Film & Television Alliance (IFTA), noted, "frequently, independent producers and distributors are hit the hardest by content theft. This agreement is a textbook example of the private sector working cooperatively to help solve a glaring economic problem while protecting consumers."

The Copyright Alert System Will Stabilize the Creative Industries

Rich Bengloff, President of American Association of Independent Music (A2IM) called it an "historic agreement that will reduce the financial distress being experienced by our independent music label community so that our members and their artists can continue to create and invest in the music they love and, in doing so, help protect thousands of musical artists and their musical compositions, across the United States."

Both the Center for Copyright Information and the Copyright Alert System are voluntary collaborations between the entertainment and broadband business communities. Participating ISPs will begin implementing Copyright Alerts in 2011 and 2012. [Editor's Note: The Copyright Alert System went into effect in February 2013.]

The companies and associations collaborating on the framework include:

- MPAA and MPAA members: Walt Disney Studios Motion Pictures; Paramount Pictures Corporation; Sony Pictures Entertainment Inc.; Twentieth Century Fox Film Corporation; Universal City Studios LLC; and Warner Bros. Entertainment Inc.

- RIAA and RIAA members: Universal Music Group Recordings, Warner Music Group, Sony Music Entertainment, and EMI Music North America.

- ISPs: AT&T, Cablevision Systems Corp., Comcast Corp., Time Warner Cable, and Verizon.

- IFTA: representing the Independent Producers & Distributors of Film & Television Programming.

- A2IM: representing their 283 music label members, small and medium sized businesses located across the United States representing many different musical genres reflective of the cultural diversity of our country.

> "Since the implementation of [their copyright alert system], music sales in France have not significantly increased, raising speculation of whether the three strikes law is deterring Internet users away from torrent sites."

The Copyright Alert System Violates Consumers' Rights and Will Not Stop Copyright Infringement

Joey LeMay

Joey LeMay is a staff writer for Mint Press, *and specializes in education and campaign coverage. In the following viewpoint, LeMay examines the Copyright Alert System, which was modeled after a similar program in France. LeMay reports that the system will provide six alerts meant to educate consumers about illegal activity over their Internet connection, such as pirating music, in hopes that consumers will self-correct the behavior. Concerns have been raised by the Electronic Frontier Foundation that this system lacks transparency and contains hidden costs, LeMay writes. The similar alert system in France has been fraught with controversy, and the fact that music sales there have not increased significantly during the three years the system has been in place, the author contends, indicates that this approach is not working.*

As you read, consider the following questions:

1. According to LeMay, what are each of the six alerts expected to be like?

2. What percentage of users hide their IP addresses using a VPN, according to a 2011 study cited by the author?

3. How much has the RIAA spent on government lobbying from 2000 to 2010, according to LeMay?

With the growing crackdown on large-scale Internet piracy and copyright protections, recent reports suggest the oft-delayed Copyright Alert System will be implemented by Internet Service Providers (ISPs) by the end of the year [2012]. [Editor's note: The system went into effect in February 2013.] The "six strike" program, as it is commonly referred to as, would make ISPs send alerts to its users if it finds the account is being misused for actions such as piracy. The foundation of the program, however, is in question as France begins quantifying the effectiveness of its three-strike program implemented in 2009.

Under the system to be implemented in the United States, a third party such as the Recording Industry Association of America (RIAA), Walt Disney Studios, Sony Pictures and other entertainment corporations would monitor file-sharing networks and collect IP addresses of those suspected of pirating and copyright infringement. The IP addresses would then be reported to their respective ISPs, which would trigger a copyright alert and begin the alert system between the ISP and user.

Jill Lesser, head of the Center for Copyright Information (CCI), told *Ars Technica* that the project was slated to be un-

The Copyright Alert System Will Not Stop Hardcore Pirates

Serious content pirates are *already* used to working around piracy reporting systems like this. They encrypt their traffic, set up seed sites outside the United States, and generally know what they're doing. The Copyright Alert System is not going to stop them or even slow them down.

The real question is how smoothly—and competently—piracy sleuths and ISPs can manage this system. If piracy reports are very accurate and ISPs actions on them consistent, the Copyright Alert System will at most be a minor annoyance for folks who are inadvertently participating in piracy, and just "business as usual" for serious pirates.

Geoff Duncan, Digital Trends, *September 14, 2012. www.digitaltrends.com.*

rolled before the end of the year after being delayed last December and this past June. She noted that the program was created with the intention of explaining to the Internet user that what they are doing is illegal.

"It is not a six strikes program," Lesser said. "This is an educational program; there are a series of educational alerts that will be sent out to subscribers."

The System Focuses on P2P Sharing

The Copyright Alert System's primary focus is peer-to-peer (P2P) file sharing, describing a network of computers where individuals can download, upload and share files found on the users' respective machines.

The Center for Copyright Information (CCI) has posed a hypothetical scenario of what each of the six alerts of the system could look like. While each alert is largely the same in its content, ISPs are allowed to word each measure as they see fit. The first alert would likely be an email notifying the user of potential misuse from their account. A second alert would simply act as a reminder to the previous message.

A third alert becomes more invasive, as an online component such as a pop-up notice or landing page would require the user to acknowledge they received the letter in order to further use the Internet. A fourth alert would rehash the language in the third while the fifth alert allows the ISP to become more hands on. The ISP would then have the jurisdiction to reduce the user's Internet speed or other measures determined by the ISP. The sixth and final alert would act as a final warning and give the ISP full authority on how to handle the situation as the user would no longer be under the Copyright Alert System.

ISP Accounts Will Not Be Cut Off

"This Copyright Alert System protects a consumer's essential services and does not, under any circumstance, require the ISP to terminate an Internet subscriber's account," CCI said. "ISPs are not required to impose any mitigation measure that could disable a subscriber's essential Internet or other services, such as telephone service (to call 911), email or security or health service."

Once a user is out of the system, however, the ISP may alter services as it sees fit, or turn the user over to authorities. CCI acknowledges that those instances would likely be rare and would only be triggered by a large-scale number of downloads or participation in pirating.

"At that point, all of the tools that the content owners and the ISPs have at their disposal are there," Lesser said. "ISPs can, and have, taken action based on that. Content owners we know have taken action against large-scale pirates."

Piracy Has Been a Problem for Years

As the Internet became the ubiquitous tool of this day and age, access to movies, music and television shows were mere clicks away. And the growing number of these Internet measures are attempting to quell the piracy of already savvy Web users, as a 2011 report found that 15 percent of P2P file-sharers have hidden their IP addresses via Virtual Private Networks (VPN) and other tactics such as proxies. In 2008, the National Cable and Telecommunications Association targeted the "theft" of online content by building the framework for a tiered system of educating about copyrighted material and reducing the influence of torrents on the entertainment industry.

The White House called the agreement between the entertainment industry and ISPs a "positive step" toward halting piracy, but that's not to say it didn't come with a little coaxing. Between 2000 and 2010, the RIAA spent more than $90 million to cover government lobbying costs and more than $50 million in legal fees challenging file sharing. Then, in August [2012], it was reported that a former RIAA lobbyist Beryl Howell was named a district judge in Washington D.C. and has handled numerous cases that pertain to copyright and ISPs.

Hidden Costs Will Trickle Down

What is equally disconcerting about Copyright Alert System is the lack of transparency and outside input into its creation, says the Electronic Frontier Foundation (EFF). While the costs of the program have not been disclosed, Parker Higgins, an activist with the EFF, said there will be a cost burden on ISPs that will eventually be felt by consumers.

"The delays are another indication that this is an expensive program that is getting passed to ISPs, and then on to the public," Higgins said. "It's a cost that we're skeptical that the American people should bear."

In France, a three strikes rule, dubbed the "HADOPI Law," was introduced in 2009 to stop Internet piracy. One of the reliable figures to study when quantifying its effect is music album sales, as music consumes a large amount of pirate activity. At the height of the Internet boom and introduction of Internet piracy, the RIAA reported a loss of album sales of 8.9 percent. RIAA contends that piracy hurts the bottom line of record companies and can shut down independent labels.

But since the implementation of HADOPI, music sales in France have not significantly increased, raising speculation of whether the three strikes law is deterring Internet users away from torrent sites. In fact, since the law's implementation, new music revenues in France are still down 3.9 percent since 2009.

> "Creative Commons licenses are the true allies of artists who are struggling for recognition and remuneration."

Creative Commons Licensing Promotes Creative Works

Glyn Moody

Glyn Moody is a technology writer whose work has been published in prominent periodicals, including Wired, The Economist, *and the* Financial Times. *In the following viewpoint, Moody argues in favor of Creative Commons licensing within the framework of refuting George Howard's blog post opposing Creative Commons. Moody maintains that Howard, like others, fundamentally misunderstands Creative Commons and its predecessor—copyleft—a movement that emerged from software design and encouraged programmers to share their work. Moody clarifies that Creative Commons supplements copyright rather than replacing it, helping unknown artists better reach and engage with audiences.*

As you read, consider the following questions:

1. According to Moody, who founded the copyleft movement and what was his job?

Glyn Moody, "Why Creative Commons Licenses Help Rather than Hinder Struggling Artists," *Techdirt*, October 31, 2011.

2. What additional permissions, according to the author, does Creative Commons allow a creator to grant to users?

3. According to Moody, how does Creative Commons provide a creator with the ability to earn income from his or her work?

Creative Commons (CC) has been with us for nearly a decade [as of 2011], so you would have thought people might understand it by now. Apparently not, judging by the title of this blog post: "How Creative Commons Can Stifle Artistic Output" [posted October 13, 2011 on the blog *TuneCore*].

The author, George Howard, begins reasonably enough:

> Now, the servicing of the muse is not compelled by money, but, rather, other impulses. However, absent some type of financial return for the artists' work, bad things happen: artists begin to believe that their work is without value, and they stop; or, artists have to subsidize their artistic income by working a soul-crushing job that eventually diminishes their ability/desire/time to create . . . and they stop. In either case, art stops being created. This to me is unacceptable. I defy anyone to give me a good argument against the creation of more art.

Clearly from that description Howard is concerned mainly with artists that are relatively unknown and/or struggling, and his point about their need to make money is a fair one. But from that premise he then makes this extraordinary leap:

> All of this is why I react negatively to proponents of the so-called "copyleft" movement.

He goes on:

> As a bit of background, the copyleft movement originated from software development, where hobbyist programmers desired to make software free (or very cheap) in order to reduce/eliminate piracy.

The Intent of Creative Commons Licensing

Say you're an independent musician. You likely want as many people as possible to hear your songs; but without a major record label to promote your recordings through the traditional channels . . . you might choose a Creative Commons license that allows you to give away some of your music for free, while reserving the right to sell your music commercially. You might even want to allow other musicians to produce remixes, as long as they credit your contribution.

Creative Commons licensing also helps end users understand exactly what they can and can't do with your work, thus resolving a major point of confusion.

Katherine Noyes, PC World, *May 23, 2010.*

Copyleft Facilitates Content Sharing

That is wrong in just about every respect. Copyleft, which actually depends upon copyright in order to work, was invented in 1983 by Richard Stallman. Far from being a "hobbyist", Stallman was one of the test programmers of his day. Moreover, copyleft—specifically the GNU General Public License— was devised not to "reduce/eliminate piracy", but almost its polar opposite: to encourage and facilitate sharing.

The author's understanding of how Creative Commons licenses work seems equally shaky:

There are several justifications for an artist or songwriter to give up copyrights. The first is reasonable: that by providing a means for artists to more easily exchange rights, reduces transaction costs, and thus encourages collaboration.

Artists employing Creative Commons licenses do not "give up copyrights": they always retain them. But they grant additional permissions to others—to share, to adapt, to sell. That's not about "exchanging rights"—there's no quid pro quo required, and rarely does this result in any artistic collaboration; instead it's from a desire to see your work enjoyed or re-used more widely.

> The second—that current copyright law enforces and encourages a restrictive permission culture to the detriment of the public good—is not. By this I mean that the idea that copyright somehow impedes creativity and artistic development is just plain wrong.

The idea that copyright on a work impedes "creativity and artistic development" refers to its effect not on the original creator, but on other artists, since by definition copyright is a monopoly that forbids them from building on the creations of others unless they ask permission—often expensive or impossible to obtain. Creative Commons licenses, by contrast, encourage this kind of activity by granting permissions upfront to everyone, making them particularly beneficial for those rising creators with limited means but plenty of ideas.

CC Licenses Promote Unknown Artists

Despite this, Howard insists the problem lies not with copyright itself, but elsewhere:

> what really impedes creativity and artistic development is the artist's perception that his or her music is valueless/the inability of the artist to monetize his or her output.

And yet it's copyright that exacerbates this perception among struggling and still unknown artists that their art is valueless, not CC licenses. Copyright places obstacles in the way of sharing your enthusiasm for a creative work by passing it on so that it can be explored and enjoyed by others. All CC licenses permit this, and it is precisely this spreading of the word that is likely to lead to the creator becoming better known and appreciated.

Nor does making works more freely available preclude the possibility of earning money from them. Fans may buy the work in other formats—for example as a book, CD or LP as well as a download. People may want to make direct contributions to support the artist to encourage them to produce more. *Techdirt* has devoted many posts to the different ways in which revenue can be generated from CC-licensed goods that are made available online.

Creative Works Are Valuable

Howard concludes:

> Artists tend to have—at best—an uncomfortable relationship with the monetization of their work, and need no encouragement to devalue it. Rather, artists need to be reminded that their contribution to this deeply troubled world is valuable. The exchange of value between an artist and his or her fans, is a means to allow the artist to continue creating art, and thus is crucial.

His own words emphasise that what is crucial is an "exchange of value between an artist and his or her fans." Copyright, with its ever-expanding range of restrictions and harsh punishments for those who overstep the mark—even unwittingly—hardly promotes that exchange. Creative Commons licenses are the true allies of artists who are struggling for recognition and remuneration, thanks to their broad permissions and explicit encouragement to share and enjoy, which promotes and enhances that exchange—and helps to generate that crucial financial return too.

| "*Copyright protection . . . legislation and litigation has helped destroy a number of innovative business models.*"

Innovate or Legislate

Reihan Salam and Patrick Ruffini

Reihan Salam is a conservative commentator who regularly writes for the National Review *and has made many appearances on television and radio. Patrick Ruffini is a conservative political strategist who specializes in media and fund-raising. In the following viewpoint, Salam and Ruffini argue that the Internet has been a boon to the US economy although the change has been difficult for many traditional industries to adjust to. They examine how Hollywood has fought back against technological advancements and strengthened copyright law in an effort to protect its own revenue stream. Piracy has continued despite this, the authors argue—that is, until forward-thinking companies develop legal business models for sharing media that shift most consumers away from pirating media that they feel entitled to. Digital streaming has also been incredibly lucrative for artists, Salam and Ruffini maintain, and the entertainment industry has grown economically, despite a worldwide recession, because of technological advancements. The authors assert that the eco-*

nomic advantages offered by the Internet could save the languishing US economy, but Hollywood and other industries must stop fighting the tide of changing technology.

As you read, consider the following questions:

1. According to the authors, citing a 2011 study, how many jobs were created for every job destroyed by the Internet?

2. How much did state-sponsored film industry tax breaks and giveaways increase between 2001 and 2010, according to Salam and Ruffini?

3. How much did household spending on entertainment in the United States increase from 2005 to 2010, according to the authors?

In 2012, a number of institutions that long defined how Americans communicated are teetering near the brink of collapse. Major newspapers in cities across the country have stopped publishing. Strip-mall anchors from Circuit City to Blockbuster to Borders have filed for Chapter 11 bankruptcy protection. The U.S. Postal Service struggles under the weight of crushing pension obligations, as e-mail, Facebook, Twitter, and Skype render it all but obsolete. In politics, traditional modes of wielding power are also being disrupted. One prominent example is the recent battle over the Stop Online Piracy Act, or SOPA, in which grassroots activists defeated once-powerful Hollywood lobbyists.

What's toppling these formerly invincible companies and institutions? In almost every case, the proximate cause is the Internet, and the disruption it has wrought on inefficient businesses in every corner of the economy. And so we are now engaged in a war over its future.

The Internet's enemies have proven vocal, organized, and effective, while the vast majority of consumers, workers, and

153

entrepreneurs it has enriched have proven anything but, and the fight over SOPA must be understood in this larger context.

A McKinsey Global Institute study published last spring found that, worldwide, 2 billion people were connected to the Internet and almost $8 trillion exchanged hands via e-commerce. The United States captures 30 percent of all the revenues generated by the global Internet economy, and 40 percent of the net income. Moreover, the Internet has been a powerful driver of economic growth and job creation. In a survey of small and medium-sized enterprises, McKinsey found that for every job destroyed by the Internet, 2.6 were created. In the advanced countries that were included in the survey, the United States among them, Internet consumption and expenditure accounted for 21 percent of economic growth over the past few years.

One is reminded of Jack Kemp's call in the 1970s and 1980s for "enterprise zones," blighted urban areas in which regulations would be eliminated, and taxes lowered, to spark entrepreneurship and growth. The Internet has been the ultimate enterprise zone. Just as Hong Kong's freedom and prosperity contrasted vividly with China's desperate poverty for much of the last century, the Internet stands out as an island of low regulation and taxation in a broader economy that grows less free with each passing year. The question is whether we will allow Internet-enabled innovation to continue transforming the economy—dramatically reducing the cost and raising the quality of our education and health sectors, for example—or, alternatively, we will allow the Internet's growth to be choked off by cronyism. . . .

For now, the Internet represents the great exception to the rising tide of state-guided capitalism, in which government favors politically connected firms and industries. As Ian Bremmer observes in his ominous book *The End of the Free Market*, the governments of the world's rising economies seek to dominate key economic sectors. The global markets for energy, aviation, shipping, power generation, arms production, telecommunications, metals, minerals, petrochemicals, and much else are increasingly being manipulated by state-owned enterprises and sovereign wealth funds.

Even the United States, long the bulwark of entrepreneurial capitalism, has moved in a dirigiste direction. During his recent State of the Union address, President Obama celebrated the bailouts of GM and Chrysler, promising that "what's happening in Detroit can happen in other industries." What happened in Detroit is that taxpayers gave a massive infusion of cash to politically connected workers and investors in a collapsing industry.

When we think of state capitalism, we tend to think of the Rust Belt, where automobile manufacturers and steel producers have been clamoring for bailouts and protective tariffs for decades. But in the 21st century, it is Hollywood that has been the most effective at securing handouts. Until 2001, only four U.S. states had programs to encourage film production, typically through tax breaks and other giveaways. That year, the total amount offered was in the neighborhood of $1 million. Between 2001 and 2010, however, the number of states offering incentives went from four to 40, and the amount offered increased to $1.4 billion—note the change from "m" to "b." Thankfully, a handful of states have abandoned their film-incentive programs since 2010, having recognized that they were a bad deal for taxpayers.

Yet film-incentive programs are just the tip of the iceberg. Hollywood has pursued a number of strategies to enrich itself at the expense of the broader public. One of the most egregious has been the ongoing extension of copyright terms.

Article I, Section 8 of the U.S. Constitution gives Congress the power "to promote the progress of science and useful arts, by securing for limited times to authors and inventors the exclusive right to their respective writings and discoveries." Congress has quietly acquiesced to several extensions of copyright terms over the past 35 years, with overwhelming bipartisan support. Only with the 1998 Sonny Bono Copyright Term Extension Act did anyone notice that these extensions weren't serving the purpose stated in the Constitution. It is one thing to offer longer copyright terms for new works "to promote the progress of science and useful arts." But to extend the copyright terms of existing works simply allows incumbent firms to extract value from old ideas whose creators expected that their copyright would expire after a "limited" time that has now passed. When asked to strike down the 1998 law, the Supreme Court declined—in an uncharacteristically literal-minded spirit, it noted that repeatedly extending copyright terms for existing works a few decades at a time does not in itself make copyright unlimited. But it should be beyond dispute that endless extensions of existing copyrights violate the spirit of the Constitution.

Among defenders of today's copyright regime, including at least some conservatives, there is a conviction that intellectual property should be protected the same way that any other kind of property would be. But this has not been the outcome. As the attorney and Bush-administration veteran Stewart Baker has argued, copyright has come to resemble "a constantly expanding government program run for the benefit of a noisy, well-organized interest group."

Before 1978, for example, one had to place a copyright notice on the title page of a book, file with the copyright office, and file to renew the copyright after 28 years, at which point the copyright term was extended for another 28 years. These requirements were hardly onerous, yet they helped manage the growth of copyright litigation by limiting copyright to those who explicitly sought its protection. Now, however, every work, including doodles sketched on a napkin, is automatically given copyright protection. This has led to an "orphan works" problem, in which works abandoned by their creators are left in legal limbo.

During the mid-1980s, Hollywood made a concerted effort to destroy the VCR on the grounds that it was designed to facilitate copyright infringement. In the end, the courts decided that because the VCR had a substantial non-infringing purpose—to shift the time when people watched television programs—its makers could not be held liable for their users' infringing activities. But in 1992, the recording industry succeeded in pushing to passage the Audio Home Recording Act, which mandated that digital-audio devices have industry-approved copyright protection built in. The new law also created a new tax on empty cassettes and other blank media, which was meant to pay for the costs of piracy. In 1997, the No Electronic Theft Act dramatically increased the statutory charges for copyright infringement and, separately, the recording industry attempted to ban MP3 players, a bid that narrowly failed.

In 1998, the Digital Millennium Copyright Act (DMCA) essentially gave the motion-picture and recording industries veto power over the design of all digital-media devices in the name of controlling piracy. The DMCA gives an organization called the DVD Copy Control Association control over the design of all DVD players; as a result, DVDs are often encoded with software that controls the viewing experience—for example, by preventing consumers from skipping commercials at the start of a film. The Prioritizing Resources and Organization for Intellectual Property Act of 2008 represented yet another expansion of copyright protection. Taken together, this wave of legislation and litigation has helped destroy a number of innovative business models, including My.MP3.com, an early-2000s service that aimed to enable consumers to listen to their own legally purchased CDs while on the road.

Copyright Law Balances Protection and Innovation

While the size and scope of current copyright violations are vastly disproportionate to anything in previous history, in the 18th century our Founding Fathers were familiar with copyright violation. In fact Great Britain was quite angry at what was perceived to be rampant theft in the colonies of their intellectual property in the form of literature.

With this in mind, our Founding Fathers wrote the clause in the Constitution on protecting content. But they knew that there was a very serious cost for this government-instituted monopoly. It is a balancing test to ensure that we have the maximum amount of productivity overall.

With no copyright protection, it was perceived that there would be insufficient incentive for content producers to create new content—without the ability to compensate them for their work. And with too much copyright protection, as in copyright protection that carried on longer than necessary for the incentive, it will greatly stifle innovation.

Derek S. Khanna, Republican Study Committee,
November 16, 2012. www.scribd.com.

And the Obama administration has greatly expanded the federal government's efforts to protect the interests of copyright holders, tasking the overburdened bureau of Immigration and Customs Enforcement with seizing foreign websites accused of copyright infringement.

Just as copyright terms have grown ever longer and more restrictive, we've seen a parallel strengthening of patent rights.

As the George Mason University economist Alex Tabarrok has argued, this has tended to reduce innovation. In *Launching the Innovation Renaissance*, Tabarrok observes that strong intellectual-property protections at times create a "resting on laurels" effect. Rather than invest in innovation to outcompete their rivals, firms stockpile patents and attack potential competitors with lawsuits. In the technology industry, billions are now being diverted from research and development to acquire patent portfolios. As Microsoft founder Bill Gates presciently warned in 1991, "I feel certain that some large company will patent some obvious thing" and use the patent to "take as much of our profits as they want." Microsoft, alas, has since played the role of the large company, as have innumerable patent trolls.

That, in essence, is where Hollywood finds itself today. As consumers and entrepreneurs seek new, more convenient ways to consume media, Hollywood is fighting desperate rearguard actions to force people to consume media in the ways it finds most congenial. The industry's prodigious success in translating glitz, glamor, and well-timed campaign contributions into political influence has lulled it into believing that the federal government can save it from the need to innovate. While Hollywood failed to ban the VCR and the MP3 player, it succeeded in suing My.MP3.com and a streaming-film service called Kaleidescape out of business.

The entertainment industry claims, and it really is true, that media piracy has increased over the last decade. Last summer, a survey sponsored by the American Assembly, a public-affairs forum affiliated with Columbia University, found that 46 percent of U.S. adults had acquired unauthorized music or video, a number that rises to 70 percent among those younger than 30. But only 2 percent acquired *most* of their media collections through piracy, and the emergence of legal streaming-music and -video services has curbed the appetite for unauthorized content. The emergence of Netflix's streaming-video service, for example, has coincided with a marked decline in the number of searches for BitTorrent, a hub for pirated media. The convenience of iTunes has similarly reduced piracy as a share of digital-media consumption. Last year, the Social Science Research Council published *Media Piracy in Emerging Economies*, the most comprehensive study of the piracy problem to date. The report, which was notably not funded by the entertainment industry, concludes that the key to curbing media piracy isn't heavy-handed legislation. Rather, it is the kind of business-model innovation that allows users to consume content conveniently and affordably.

It's understandable that big media companies are reluctant to embrace business-model innovation, since the old model was incredibly lucrative for them. Joe Karaganis, a leading expert on media piracy based at American Assembly, observes that while the transition from CDs to MP3s has dramatically reduced distribution costs for the major record labels, they've until recently resisted returning more of the wholesale price to artists—who make the same 15 to 20 percent on wholesale that they did before the collapse of distribution costs—or cutting retail prices for consumers. A number of indie labels and digital-streaming services, in contrast, return 50 to 90 percent of the wholesale price to artists. It is hardly surprising that consumers and artists have been flocking to streaming-music services such as Spotify, which has just reached 3 million members—they offer a much better deal to artist and consumer alike by eliminating the middleman, which is exactly what the Internet does best.

Michael Masnick, a blogger and venture capitalist who has taken a leading role in technology-policy debates, recently released a report on how the rise of digital consumption has changed the entertainment industry—and his core finding is that the entertainment industry is booming. Between 2005 and 2010, the global music industry increased in value from $132 billion to $168 billion. Despite a weak economy, the share of total household spending devoted to entertainment increased by 15 percent in the U.S. over the same period. Employment in the U.S. entertainment industry increased by 20 percent from the late 1990s to the late 2000s, in part because of an explosion of activity that occurred outside the largest media companies.

The entertainment industry relies heavily on the notion that artists have been devastated by increasing piracy. Yet it turns out that only legacy media firms that are reluctant to embrace the digital revolution have been hurt; artists willing to adapt to the new environment, and to the desire of consumers for a more direct relationship with the artists they admire, have flourished. According to the Bureau of Labor Statistics, the number of independent artists increased by 43 percent from 1998 to 2008 as it grew easier to make a living without being signed by a major recording company. This has proven particularly advantageous for artists who appeal to culturally conservative consumers, a market niche that the big media companies have largely ignored.

Essentially, those companies are trying to enlist the federal government in an effort to save their failing business model, under the pretense of looking out for artists and workers. It would be far more accurate to say that digital consumption has benefited artists and workers as well as consumers. But like the Big Three, Big Media wants a bailout. And until recently, it had reason to think it would get its wish. After all, it has managed to deploy government power against a number of similarly promising Web-based technologies. Hollywood contributes vast sums to political candidates, particularly on the left, through the Motion Picture Association of America and Recording Industry Association of America, both powerful lobbies. For decades they won almost every political battle they joined, in part because they tended to strike deals behind closed doors. The winning streak, however, has come to an end.

At the outset of the most recent legislative debate over on-line piracy, Hollywood was poised to extend its flawless copyright-expansion win streak. Under the guise of blocking foreign "rogue" websites, the Protect IP Act, or PIPA, an earlier Senate counterpart to SOPA, achieved levels of bipartisan co-sponsorship unseen in all but 19 other bills out of the 1,900 the current Senate had considered as of November, according to OpenCongress.org. In May 2011, the legislation passed the Judiciary Committee by voice vote, without hearings. There was no reason to think that the House version, which became SOPA, would be any different.

But when House Judiciary Committee chairman Lamar Smith (R., Texas) delivered a bill in late October, alarm bells went off in start-ups and venture-capital firms throughout Silicon Valley and New York City. Brad Burnham, a co-founder of Union Square Ventures and the first institutional investor in Twitter, helped mobilize the early protests, which would inspire the larger blackouts of Wikipedia, Reddit, and more than 100,000 other websites in January of this year. "The infrastructure of the Internet, chips, routers, and microprocessors were conceived and created a long way from Washington, and the entrepreneurs and investors who built those businesses liked it that way," Burnham reflected. "Politics had little impact on this insulated world." But slumber was no longer an option: An industry that had shunned lobbyists now paid the price in legislation that placed in legal jeopardy the business model of allowing users to freely share content without pre-screening or approval—the basis of the modern Internet. (The original version of SOPA would have criminalized sites' taking "deliberate actions to avoid confirming a high probability" of copyright violations.)

That Congress was blithely preparing to regulate an industry it did not understand was on full display in December's House mark-up hearings, at which proponents of SOPA professed ignorance of the workings of the Domain Name System, a fundamental piece of Internet architecture that SOPA proposed radically to alter. North Carolina Democrat Mel Watt, an early sponsor of the bill, made the memorable confession "I'm not a nerd."

To the tech community, stopping SOPA would become a life-or-death struggle. On top of its censorship provisions, SOPA sought to give copyright holders the right to sue U.S.-based websites; it also would have required that search engines censor results pointing to sites that had been accused of piracy and granted legal immunity to Internet-service providers that voluntarily shut off access to websites suspected of piracy.

Ultimately, the indictment of SOPA as a complex regulatory boondoggle may prove more instrumental to its collapse than have been the Internet's cries of censorship. So suggests Republican lawmakers' decision to dump the billen masse.

Like most examples of Beltway cronyism, SOPA was the product of an out-of-touch bipartisan lobbyist elite, and it understood precious little about the networked and decentralized medium it proposed to regulate. This elite badly underestimated the political power of an "Internet public" connected by social media and smartphones. A guerrilla force of techies and populists, ranging across the political spectrum from MoveOn.org to the Tea Party Patriots, joined forces to mount an unconventional assault on Hollywood's lobbying arm, which had spent $94 million lobbying for copyright legislation in 2011. The result: the January 18 Web blackout that prompted millions of calls to Capitol Hill, forced dozens of lawmakers to switch sides, and consigned SOPA to the dustbin of history—for now.

After both sides of the SOPA debate had been heard, it was conservatives who were quicker to rally to the side of the rebels. At one point hours into the Internet blackout, 26 of the 29 legislators who had switched sides were Republicans. Minnesota Democrat Al Franken, who had fashioned himself the Senate's chief defender of the "open Internet," would go on to send an e-mail message to supporters defending the Protect IP Act in the name of "middle class workers—most of them union workers" who work in industries that depend on intellectual-property law. Franken, himself a card-carrying member of the Screen Actors Guild, represented in microcosm the coalition of Hollywood and labor threatened by the disruptive forces of technology. Senators Chuck Schumer and Kirsten Gillibrand, both New York Democrats, privately seethed at Republicans who withdrew their co-sponsorship, among them Florida Republican senator Marco Rubio.

Behind the scenes, Republicans were using the piracy debate to register their displeasure at Harry Reid and his imperious management of the Senate. When Reid put the Protect IP Act on the Senate floor schedule, the bill's main Republican proponents were not even consulted. A few days before the scheduled floor vote, a group of Republican senators, including chief Republican sponsor Chuck Grassley and Utah conservative Mike Lee, called upon Reid to delay consideration of the bill indefinitely.

Republican opposition to SOPA, though influenced by many factors, is rooted in conservative skepticism about the imposition of regulations rigged to favor powerful corporate insiders. This skepticism wasn't on display for most of the Bush era, when many in the GOP reconciled themselves to being part of a pro-business rather than a pro-market and pro-freedom political movement. Public hostility to the Wall Street bailouts and the rise of the Tea Party provided a useful corrective, and conservatives in Congress now wish to be on the side of consumers and the entrepreneurs who serve them, rather than that of crony capitalists who use state power to extract rents.

The Internet Threatens Traditional Commerce

It is not just media companies that seek to stifle Internet innovation. It is every established industry that fears disruptive change and wants to build protective barriers against Internet-enabled competition. Real-estate agents, mass-transit agencies, cab companies, and purveyors of wines and spirits are just a few of the special interests that have tried to regulate away competition from Web entrepreneurs.

Perhaps the most important example of an industry that fears the Internet and seeks to contain its power is the education sector. Across the country, teachers' unions have fought bitterly against online-education efforts that promise to lower the cost and improve the quality of instruction. Traditional colleges and universities have been waging rear-guard actions against online universities that do things such as offer "all you can eat" pricing plans, which allow students to take as many courses as they can handle for a flat fee. The medical profession, similarly, has been reluctant to embrace Internet-enabled technologies that empower patients and in the process drive down costs. These are the sectors most plagued by inefficiency, those in which political imperatives trump market competition more often than not. Fortunes are made in health care and education not by meeting the needs of consumers, but by securing political favors.

Economic Freedom for Everyday People

The Internet represents a radical alternative to crony capitalism. Larry Downes, a right-leaning technology analyst and one of the most insightful chroniclers of the fight against SOPA, has described what he calls "the political philosophy of the Internet": "Its central belief is the power of innovation to make things better, and its major tenet is a ruthless economic principle that treats information as currency, and sees any obstacle to its free flow as inefficient friction to be engineered out of existence." This belief is rooted in the open, meritocratic nature of the Internet itself. And it is a belief that is very much in keeping with core conservative values.

The Internet, and the phenomenal success of technology entrepreneurs such as Steve Jobs, Mark Zuckerberg, Sergey

Brin, and Larry Page, and countless others, is a vivid example of markets at their best. The world's most deregulated industry has, not coincidentally, seen corporate empires rise and fall with astonishing speed. Yet the chief beneficiaries haven't been Silicon Valley billionaires. Rather, they've been citizens, workers, and consumers who've been given the power to choose something other than the status quo.

We have described the Internet as our Hong Kong, our beacon of economic freedom. But whereas the Mainland swallowed up Hong Kong, there is a chance that the dynamism of the Internet could take over and revitalize our overtaxed, overregulated, moribund economy. Let's not blow it.

Periodical and Internet Sources Bibliography

The following articles have been selected to supplement the diverse viewpoints presented in this chapter.

Priya Barnes	"The Prospects for Protecting News Content Under the Digital Millennium Copyright Act," *Journal for Sports and Entertainment Law*, March 2012.
BBC News	"Law Relaxed on Digital Copying," December 20, 2012. www.bbc.co.uk.
Billboard	"Court Rules for Ray Charles' Children in Copyright Lawsuit (Updated)," January 29, 2013.
Kevin Collier	"Finland Is Crowdsourcing Its New Copyright Law," *Daily Dot*, January 23, 2013. www.daily dot.com.
Sean F	"SXSW Interactive Panel Blasts Copyright Law, Entertainment Industry," *Digital Digest*, March 12, 2013. www.digital-digest.com.
Timothy B. Lee	"Copyright Enforcement and the Internet: We Just Haven't Tried Hard Enough?," ArsTechnica, February 14, 2012. http://arstechnica.com.
Lucas McMaster	"Academic Senate Warns Professors About Violating Copyright Law," *Daily 49er*, March 17, 2013. www.daily49er.com.
Brendan Sasso	"Copyright Chief Calls for Crackdown on Illegal Streaming," *The Hill*, March 20, 2013.
David Savage	"Supreme Court Issues Major Copyright Ruling on Foreign Sales," *Los Angeles Times*, March 19, 2013.
Ryan Whitwam	"Comcast's Six Strikes Punishment Hijacks Your Browser," Geek, February 28, 2013. www .geek.com.

OPPOSING
VIEWPOINTS®
SERIES

CHAPTER 4

How Does Technology Affect Copyright Infringement?

Chapter Preface

In October 2012, the Librarian of Congress, who is responsible for determining exemptions from the Digital Millennium Copyright Act (DMCA) every three years, announced that unlocking a cell phone so that it can be used on any communications carrier would be illegal in 2013. This change in law angered many consumers—and even garnered criticism from the White House—which serves as evidence of American's expectation of consumer freedom. According to LiveScience's report of the change in exemptions, unlocking a cell phone is thinly protected against by the DMCA. Digital advocacy group Electronic Frontier Foundation (EFF), according to TechNewsDaily, maintains that the DMCA does not protect cell phones from being unlocked and therefore is not under the jurisdiction of the Librarian of Congress; EFF argues that the legality of unlocking cell phones must be determined by the courts. Derek Khanna, writing for the *Atlantic Monthly* in January 2013, protested that the power to send people to prison for committing a crime is not within the scope of the Librarian of Congress, who is not an elected official. Khanna also found fault with the high fines for this crime—$500,000 to $1,000,000 and/or jail time of five to ten years. The EFF points out that the DMCA's ban on unlocking cell phones is not as dire as it sounds because carriers are unlikely to pursue individuals "RIAA-style" (referring to the Recording Industry Association of America's aggressive pursuit of individuals who illegally downloaded music) and instead will focus litigation against businesses that unlock phones for commercial benefit.

"Jailbreaking" and "rooting" are terms with similar intent, but refer specifically to cracking a smartphone's software to make it possible to use programs and features that have been locked down by the manufacturer or service provider. Jailbreaking and rooting also involve circumventing digital rights management (DRM) and are known in the software security field as privilege escalation because the hacker is gaining deeper access, or privilege, than he or she would normally have. Due to an intentionally lapsed DMCA exemption, jailbreaking or rooting a smartphone (but not a tablet) is legal until at least 2015, if frustrating for service providers who have customized their phones' functionality with specific marketing intents. Cell phone companies have fought back by releasing software patches that override the privilege escalation, but hackers render patches useless within days of their release.

Of course everything can change in 2016, after the Librarian of Congress determines what exemptions to the DMCA will apply for the next three years. Without a doubt, the biggest unknown in the puzzle of copyright law during the twenty-first century is the rapidly changing technology. Even as digital media has made infringement easier, it has also opened up businesses to new ways of making money and combating the loss (perceived or real) of infringed content. The authors of the viewpoints in the following chapter debate the many-faceted question of how technology affects copyright infringement.

> "P2P programs . . . have spawned an unprecedented era of rampant and pervasive copyright infringement."

Peer-to-Peer Services Facilitate Copyright Infringement

Kollin J. Zimmermann

Kollin J. Zimmermann is an intellectual property lawyer. In the following viewpoint, he discusses the definition of distribution in copyright infringement cases. According to the author, the prevalent theory supported by legal precedent is "actual transfer," where a literal exchange of property must be demonstrated. Zimmermann maintains that this theory is too restrictive because peer-to-peer (P2P) technology is specifically designed to avoid a direct connection between those who make copyright material freely available and those who illegally download the same material. Therefore, he argues, the "making available" theory of distribution should be upheld in courts and, better yet, legislated by Congress.

As you read, consider the following questions:

1. According to Zimmermann, how many songs are being downloaded with P2P software per month?

2. In what case did an appellate court use the "making available" theory to support its finding of copyright infringement by a library, according to the author?

3. Why does Zimmermann feel that the definition of "distribute" used by the courts to support "actual transfer" theory in the *Thomas* decision is flawed?

Peer-to-peer (P2P) file sharing software of one type or another has been downloaded worldwide over 600,000,000 times. These programs, such as Gnutella, KaZaA, and BitTorrent, allow users to copy and transfer copyrighted music from one user to another, free of charge. While P2P programs represent a significant and beneficial technological achievement, they also have spawned an unprecedented era of rampant and pervasive copyright infringement of musical works. The International Federation of the Phonographic Industry (IFPI) has stated that the ratio of unauthorized to authorized music downloads is more than 40:1. Although iTunes, the leading authorized online music distributor, has sold over six billion songs, it has been estimated that P2P file sharing accounts for over four billion songs a month—a ratio of approximately 150:1.

The Music Industry Has Suffered

As a result of this unauthorized mass distribution of songs, the music industry has suffered financially. From the year 2000 to the end of 2007, compact disc (CD) album sales dropped 46 percent and CD singles sales all but disappeared, declining 92 percent. From a monetary perspective, the Institute for Policy Innovation has estimated that illegal file sharing causes $12.5 billion of economic loss every year.

In 2003, seeking legal recourse, the Recording Industry Association of America (RIAA)—the trade association representing the US recording industry—began filing copyright infringement lawsuits against individual users of P2P programs.

To date, the RIAA has sued over 18,000 individual users of P2P programs for copyright infringement. Although the RIAA has stated that it plans to discontinue filing suits against individual infringers [which it did], it also stated that it will continue to pursue those cases already in progress, and it still may decide to sue particularly egregious infringers. (Although the RIAA is probably the most prominent litigant of P2P-based lawsuits, many other copyright owners have pursued similar claims, and this article is equally applicable to those cases as well.)

The RIAA's claims are based on the Copyright Act of 1976. The Copyright Act grants copyright holders six exclusive rights. One of these is the exclusive right "to distribute copies or phonorecords of the copyrighted work to the public by sale or other transfer of ownership, or by rental, lease, or lending." This is commonly known as the "exclusive right of distribution."

Theories of Distribution

There is an ongoing debate in the legal community as to what constitutes a direct violation of a copyright holder's exclusive right of distribution. On one side, there are those who argue that merely offering to distribute a copy of a copyrighted work violates this exclusive right. This is referred to as the "making available" theory. The "making available" theory is based on two main arguments. One argument is that because it is extremely difficult for copyright owners to prove that a P2P user actually distributed a song to another user, the act of making the song available for others to download should be sufficient to constitute a violation of the distribution right. The other argument is that the United States' international treaty obligations require US law to provide copyright owners with the exclusive right to make their works available to the public, and therefore the distribution right should be interpreted to encompass this right.

On the other side of the debate, there are those who argue that an actual transfer of the copyrighted work must take place for a violation of the distribution right to occur. This is known as the "actual transfer" theory. The main argument in support of the "actual transfer" theory is that the plain meaning of the term "distribute" requires an actual transfer of ownership from one person to another, and it is beyond the courts' constitutional authority to change the face and effect of the plain meaning of the statute to include a "making available" right.

The "Actual Transfer" Theory

While the debate is far from being settled, the current trend in the law is in favor of the "actual transfer" theory. This is because in the two main cases that actually have litigated this issue on the merits, the court adopted the "actual transfer" theory.

This current trend poses a serious threat to copyright owners' ability to protect their creative works from copyright infringement. Due to advances in P2P technology, it is very difficult for a rights owner to provide evidence that a P2P user actually transferred a song to another user. Without such evidence, if a court adopts the "actual transfer" theory, the rights owner may be effectively incapable of proving its case. This is a significant problem because if copyright owners are incapable of enforcing their copyright rights, then they will be less able to profit from their creative works; and if they cannot profit from their works, there will be less incentive to create those works in the first place. . . .

An Ordinary Definition

Advocates of the "actual transfer" theory argue that for a violation of the distribution right to occur, an actual transfer of the copyrighted work must take place. In the P2P context, there have been only two cases in which this issue actually was

Users Do Not Take Infringement Seriously

Besides copyright reform, the emergence of peer-to-peer networks presents us with considerable ethical challenges. Defining acceptable use, assigning liabilities, and establishing acceptable punishments for misuse all pose legal and ethical questions that we need to answer. Given the large amount of peer-to-peer traffic that is infringing copyright, there seems to be a large disconnect between acceptable social norms and legal behavior. The content industry is trying to reduce this disconnect through aggressive advertising campaigns, including messages on DVD informing customers that illegal downloads are a crime. But the fact that peer-to-peer traffic persists tends to show this education strategy is not successful, as most users remain unconvinced that copyright infringement is a serious offense. Even if we agree that copyright infringement is a criminal offense, we have shown that peer-to-peer networks involve a large number of actors, besides end users, that stand to indirectly profit from infringement. Who should then be held liable?

Nicolas Christin, Information Assurance and Security Ethics in Complex Systems, *2010.*

litigated on the merits, and in both cases, the court adopted the "actual transfer" theory. In addition, renowned copyright scholar William Patry supports the "actual transfer" theory.

Advocates of the actual transfer theory base their argument on the plain meaning rule of statutory interpretation. According to the plain meaning rule, if a statute is unambiguous, then the court should give effect to its plain, ordinary meaning. Applying this rule, the court in *Capital Records, Inc.*

v. Thomas explained, "The ordinary dictionary meaning of the word 'distribute' necessarily entails a transfer of ownership or possession from one person to another." Therefore, giving effect to the plain meaning of [section] 106(3) requires a rejection of the argument that merely making a copyrighted work available to the public is sufficient to violate the distribution right.

Important Policy Considerations

The plain meaning rule is supported by important policy considerations—namely, ensuring that citizens are able to rely on what the law, as commonly understood, says is crucial to maintaining the fabric of society. Many believe that if courts continuously deviate from the plain meaning of statutory terms, people will lose faith in the legitimacy and consistency of the judicial system. In addition, increasing the scope of copyright protection to include not only actual transfers of a copyright work, but also the mere making available of a copyrighted work, would be a significant substantive change in the law. As such, many people believe these types of changes are best left to the legislature, not the courts. Balancing society's interest in providing incentives for people to innovate with society's interest in disseminating information to the public is a difficult and complicated endeavor. Congress, with its vast resources and its political connection to the public at large, is best suited for this task. Therefore, per the "actual transfer" theory, courts should apply the plain, ordinary meaning of the term "distribute," and they should leave substantive changes in the scope of copyright protection to the democratic process.

Actual Transfer Theory Is Ambiguous

While the arguments in favor of the "actual transfer" theory appear to be persuasive, there are two main criticisms of the "actual transfer" theory. First, it is based on a faulty premise. The plain meaning rule should be applied only if the statute is unambiguous, and the definition of "distribute" is ambiguous. The court in *Thomas* cited the *Merriam-Webster's Collegiate Dictionary* for the definition, "to give out or deliver," but had the court chosen a different dictionary, it may have reached a different conclusion. For example, the *Cambridge Advanced Learner's Dictionary* defines "distribute" as "to supply for sale," and the *Webster's New Collegiate Dictionary* defines the term as "to supply." Because it is possible to supply something without actually transferring it to another person, these definitions call into question the "plain meaning" of the term distribute. Accordingly, because there is more than one reasonable interpretation of the term "distribute," the term cannot be considered unambiguous, and therefore the plain meaning rule should not apply.

Keeping Pace with Technology

Another criticism of the "actual transfer" theory is that by narrowly interpreting the term "distribute" to include only actual transfers of copyrighted works, courts are limiting the scope of copyright protection unnecessarily and unwisely in a time when the legal system is racing to keep pace with rapid advances in technology. While perhaps, as a general rule, broadening the scope of a statute should be left to Congress, in the high technology industry of P2P file sharing, courts should use what little leeway they have in order to keep up with modern times. Ultimately, Congress should be the one to create new statutes in order to combat new threats, but the legislative process can be extremely slow, and by the time a bill is passed, the technology might have changed already. Therefore, in the face of rapid advances in P2P technology, courts should not hesitate to interpret the Copyright Act in a way that adequately addresses these new concerns.

The "Making Available" Theory

Advocates of the "making available" theory argue that the act of making a copyrighted work available to the public is sufficient to constitute a violation of the distribution right. The main proponent of the "making available" theory is the RIAA. A few courts, however, as well as US Copyright Office General Counsel David O. Carson and [expert] Professor David Nimmer, support the "making available" theory.

There are three main arguments for why courts should adopt the "making available" theory. First, in the legislative history of the Copyright Act of 1976, Congress appeared to treat the term "publication" as synonymous with "distribution," and the Copyright Act defines "publication" to include "offers to distribute." Second, courts should adopt the making available theory for equitable reasons—namely, the inability of copyright owners to prove that a P2P user actually transferred the copyrighted work. Finally, many believe the United States' international treaty obligations require the courts to adopt the making available theory.

A Logical Fallacy

Although the Copyright Act of 1976 does not define "distribution," it does define "publication." "Publication" is defined in the Copyright Act as either "the distribution of copies or phonorecords of a work to the public by sale or other transfer of ownership, or by rental, lease, or lending," or alternatively "the offering to distribute copies or phonorecords to a group of persons for purposes of further distribution, public performance, or public display." This is significant because in the legislative history of the Copyright Act, Congress seemed to treat the term "distribution" as synonymous with the term "publication," often using the two terms interchangeably. Therefore, when looking for the appropriate definition of "distribution," courts should turn to the definition of "publication" and conclude that "distribution" includes making copyrighted works available to the public (i.e., offering to distribute copyrighted works).

In response to this argument, Patry and a few courts have explained that equating "publication" with "distribution" is a classic example of the logical fallacy known as "affirming the consequent." This fallacy is illustrated as follows: if X, then Y; Y, therefore X. Put in context, this means that just because all "distributions" are "publications" does not mean that all "publications" are "distributions." Furthermore, the mere fact that the legislative history refers to the two terms interchangeably does not mean necessarily that that the two terms are in fact interchangeable. Congress specifically chose to define "publication," and it chose not to define "distribution." If Congress wanted the definition of "publication" to apply to "distribution" as well, it could have written that in the statute, but it chose not to do so. Accordingly, critics note that courts should hesitate before inferring a congressional intent to equate the two terms when there is nothing in the statute supporting such an instruction.

The *Hotaling* Case

In *Hotaling v. Church of Latter Day Saints*, the Fourth Circuit addressed the "making available" issue in a non-P2P context. In *Hotaling*, the defendant, a church library, made unauthorized copies of Hotaling's copyrighted work and made them available to the public. The district court granted the defendant's motion for summary judgment because there was no evidence showing specific instances in which the library actually loaned the infringing copies to members of the public. The appellate court, however, reversed the lower court's decision and explained that if a plaintiff were required to show that there had been an actual act of distribution, then he would be "prejudiced by a library that does not keep records of public use, and the library would unjustly profit by its own omission." Accordingly, based on equitable concerns regarding the difficulty of proving actual distribution, the court held, "[w]hen a public library adds a work to its collection, lists the work in its index or catalog system, and makes the work available to the borrowing or browsing public, it has completed all the steps necessary for distribution to the public."

"Making Available" Should Apply

Advocates of the "making available" theory argue that the Fourth Circuit's holding is directly applicable to the RIAA's predicament, and therefore the same reasoning should apply. Just as the plaintiff in *Hotaling* was unable to prove that an actual transfer of the copyrighted work took place, the RIAA is equally incapable of doing so. As discussed previously, some courts hold that the evidence obtained by MediaSentry is insufficient to prove a violation of the distribution right because a copyright owner's agent cannot infringe the owner's own copyright rights. Furthermore, even in those jurisdictions in which MediaSentry's evidence would be sufficient, those users distributing files through BitTorrent effectively are insulated from liability because of the way BitTorrent operates. Accordingly, just as the Fourth Circuit held that when a public library adds a work to its collection and makes the work available to the public, it has completed all the steps necessary for distribution, so too should courts hold likewise when addressing this issue in the P2P context. That is, when a P2P user makes a copyrighted work available for other users to download, that "making available" should be sufficient to violate the distribution right.

The RIAA Is Not Trying Hard Enough

Advocates of the "actual transfer" theory respond to this argument by stating that the general trend, as evidenced by the decisions in *Howell* and *Thomas*, is in favor of allowing MediaSentry's evidence to be used to prove violations of the distribution right, and therefore the RIAA's inability to prove its case in that respect is unfounded. In regard to the RIAA's inability to prove its case because of programs such as BitTorrent and other advances in P2P technology, some argue that the RIAA is simply not trying hard enough. These advocates argue that there are "several organizations such as BigChampagne, NPD, BayTSP, and the investigator hired in the *Thomas* case, (which) all claim to possess expertise in tracking file-sharing traffic." Accordingly, courts should not be so quick to relieve the RIAA of the burden of proving actual distribution when there is significant evidence that the RIAA is perfectly capable of proving its case on its own. . . .

The Law Has Been Slow to Keep Up

Peer-to-peer file sharing programs are a beneficial technological advancement, but the law has been slow to keep up, and this has cost copyright owners hundreds of millions of dollars. The debate over the "making available" theory and the "actual transfer" theory marks an opportunity for courts to adapt the Copyright Act of 1976 to the year 2012. While significant, substantive changes in the scope of copyright law must come from Congress; interpreting an ambiguous statute to allow copyright holders the opportunity to defend their intellectual property rights better would not amount to judicial lawmaking. Given the equitable concerns regarding the RIAA's inability to prove that a P2P user actually transferred a song to another user, as well the United States' international obligations to provide copyright owners with an exclusive right to make their works available to the public, adopting the "making available" theory is the best course of action. Accordingly, when faced with this issue, courts should reject the "actual transfer" theory, adopt the "making available" theory, and further the constitutionally mandated policy goal of intellectual property law—promoting the creation of artistic and literary works.

> "P2P technology will . . . help legitimate efforts to offer free and inexpensive ways to legally access content."

Peer-to-Peer Services Can Be Legitimized

Devindra Hardawar

Devindra Hardawar is a technology and film blogger. In the following viewpoint, he outlines legitimate uses of peer-to-peer (P2P) software, showing how this powerful technology goes beyond the illegal trafficking in copyrighted content. For example, Hardawar writes, Adobe added P2P multicasting to its Flash video player to reduce the burden on computer networks and servers when broadcasting for a large event. Hardawar also points to the free streaming music service Spotify and World of Warcraft update distribution as legitimate uses of P2P—and considers it ironic that P2P can solve the very problem it is accused of enabling.

As you read, consider the following questions:

1. To which version of Flash player did Adobe add P2P multicasting, according to the author?

2. What smaller BitTorrent site went completely legitimate and removed all torrents that violated copyright, according to Hardawar?

3. According to Hardawar, what applications is Spotify most closely related to?

In the past few weeks [November–December 2009], there have been some major shifts in the BitTorrent community which have had a resounding impact on the larger world of peer-to-peer (P2P) file sharing. They've led to some of the largest BitTorrent sites completely changing focus, or figuring out smarter ways to continue sharing files illegally.

Meanwhile, Adobe announced a massively interesting inclusion in their upcoming Flash player 10.1 update—a seemingly innocuous version number that is adding some world-changing P2P technology to Flash video streaming.

I'd like to discuss these opposing trends of illegal versus more legitimate uses of P2P technology, and what they ultimately mean for how we use the Web.

The Times Are A-Changin'

First, The Pirate Bay shut down their tracker for good. The site used to boast having "the world's largest Bittorrent tracker," but is now opting for a different approach.

The Pirate Bay is using a combination of DHT (a decentralized P2P network) and PEX (peer exchange, a method for gathering peers) to share files directly between peers without the use of a traditional tracker. They're also doing away with torrent files by offering "magnet links", which send torrent data directly to BitTorrent clients.

Mininova, another popular BitTorrent site, recently announced that they're going completely legit by removing all of their copyright-violating torrents. Mininova has historically been more cooperative with authorities when it came to cracking down on copyright infringement, but such a drastic move from them is still surprising.

The fate of these two BitTorrent mainstays is a direct response to recent legal pressure, and it's also telling for the future of the protocol. One gives up illicit activities completely, and the other finds a way to further remove themselves from blame. Honestly, I'm not sure how long The Pirate Bay can keep up their efforts without going completely private, especially if smaller BitTorrent sites are forced to go legitimate like Mininova.

Overall, legitimacy seems to be the wisest course of action for BitTorrent sites that don't want to be as confrontational as The Pirate Bay. It also falls in line with the changing tide we've been seeing with commercial use of P2P techniques for the past few years. Gone are the days when P2P just referred to illicit file sharing. Now, many companies are relying on P2P networking as a key component of their products.

Adobe and Spotify Legitimize P2P

In short, multicasting is the notion of distributing one piece of content from one source to many destinations—all without the load of delivering it to everyone requesting it. On large local networks—streaming a corporate event, for example—this often occurs right at the routers. With Flash player 10.1, Adobe is making it possible for content distributors to multicast content by having viewers transparently share the stream.

According to Adobe, this will allow Flash video streams for huge events with millions of viewers—even for something as large as the US presidential inauguration. Flash player 10.1 will also allow developers to build more traditional P2P applications within the browser, or as a standalone application via Adobe Air.

One of the most hotly anticipated services for many music lovers is Spotify, a currently [as of late 2009] Europe-only service that utilizes P2P to allow users to instantly stream music. The Spotify application looks like a cousin to iTunes with Napster as another close relative, as it should—the service marries the desire for free tunes with the legitimacy of iTunes.

The best explanation I've found for Spotify's P2P tech comes courtesy of Wikipedia:

> The contents of each client's cache is summarized in an index which is sent to the Spotify stream hub upon connecting to the service. This index is then used to inform other clients about additional peers they can connect to for fetching streamed data for individual tracks being played. This is accommodated by each client, upon startup, acting as a server listening for incoming connections from other Spotify users, as well as intuitively connecting to other users to exchange cached data as appropriate.

P2P Is Useful

For years now, Blizzard has been using BitTorrent to distribute updates for World of Warcraft, and let's not forget how useful it is for downloading large files like Linux disk images. The struggling video service Joost also relied on P2P to distribute its content with its initial desktop application, though they have since done away with P2P to focus on streaming Flash directly from their site. (The Flash player 10.1 update should be a huge boon to them.)

While broadband speeds are increasing worldwide, there will still be many reasons to adopt P2P methods for distributing content in the future. Primarily, it severely reduces the bandwidth load for content distributors, and it prevents the danger of overloaded servers for important events. For users, it means more reliable content delivery overall (since there may be no single point of failure), and reduced costs since content providers are saving money as well.

There's no denying that illegal uses of BitTorrent and other P2P technologies will continue, but on the other hand P2P technology will also help legitimate efforts to offer free and inexpensive ways to legally access content. Spotify, for example, could make many users give up illegal music downloading due to its convenience and ease of use.

As legitimate means of accessing content become more widely available, many users will find less reason to pirate. How ironic it is that P2P, once seen merely as the source of content providers' woes, could potentially be their savior.

> *"Ebooks will continue to attract the dregs of the cybercrime underworld . . . [and are being] manipulated on a grand scale."*

Self-Published E-books Encourage Copyright Infringement

Mike Essex

Mike Essex is an online marketing manager for digital marketing agency Koozai Ltd. In the following viewpoint, Essex examines the grey area of private label rights (PLR) content and how it affects the e-book market. Many people wishing to make money with little effort buy this royalty-free licensed content and repackage it as e-books, Essex reports. Unfortunately, there are issues with quality as well as copyright infringement, Essex explains, when these "authors" stray into republishing other people's original work as their own. Distributor-publishers like Lulu and Smashwords, Essex maintains, have been able to control these quality issues to some extent with lengthy review processes; however, Amazon takes a different, more lenient approach, resulting in a higher number of low-quality and plagiarized e-books in the Kindle market. There is no ready solution to this issue of low-quality e-books, Essex concludes, but distributors are working to tighten the net and prevent criminal behavior and low quality.

As you read, consider the following questions:

1. What steps did SKS Perry have to go through to get his plagiarized book removed from Amazon, according to Essex?

2. According to Essex, what did Smashwords do to reach a distribution agreement with Barnes and Noble?

3. What are distributors like Lulu and Smashwords doing to improve the quality of their offerings and keep out stolen content, according to the author?

With Google clamping down on content farms,[1] the attention of those looking to get rich quickly from churning out content is now turning to major ebook retailers—and to selling stolen and replicated content.

A key starting point of the problem is Private Label Rights content (PLR), which allows anyone to buy prewritten content in bulk that they can then make into ebooks or website content. PLR seller Ronnie Nijmeh of PLR.me describes it as "royalty-free content, which means, when you pay for a licence, you get the rights to use the content without royalty in nearly any way you please." We might be familiar with that in photographs—the stock photo—but when it comes to words, the idea of reusing them is less well-known. But the explosion in the number of ebook readers has made such reuse suddenly attractive to some.

Royalty-Free Content Creates Quality Issues

Mark Coker, the founder of Smashwords, an ebook distributor, sees PLR as "one of the worst threats to ebooks today." It's

1. Content farms are companies that employ writers to generate high-volume textual content to increase traffic to websites and generate advertising revenue.

an easy system to get involved in as well, and "idiots fall prey to the PLR schemes and pay their $24.95 a month or whatever to access vast databases of generic content, and they have the ability to mix and match this content and republish it as an ebook in their own name."

This isn't an issue only observed by Smashwords, with AJ McDonald of Lulu, a print and digital book distributor, experiencing similar problems. "A growing concern in the ebook space is the publishing of public domain content. Sites such as Project Gutenberg and Wikipedia make it very possible for potential authors to grab works and [legally] republish them as their own," says McDonald. In the commercial market of ebooks this raises customer concerns over just what is good content, and which books are nothing more than amalgamated online information.

PLR Encourages Copyright Infringement

Vanessa Reece of Geekette Marketing, an author developing her own set of PLR, agrees that it is easy to find and to buy. "There are tonnes of places to find free, paid and limited edition PLR online. You only have to type 'PLR' and the subject you need into Google."

One prolific author of the type of content highlighted by Coker publishes "a mix of both PLR content and stolen content."

In some cases, the person simply smudged out the author name from the book cover image and didn't even bother to enter his own. Other research has highlighted Manuel Ortiz Braschi, the creator of 2,879 PLR ebooks and republished public domain content. Doing so is legal; the question is whether it's useful, given that it exists for free online already.

Although PLR.me goes through multiple editors and checks when writing its own content (including fact checking and grammar checks) the problems seem to occur after the PLR has been sold. Numerous people can buy the same packs,

Spammers and Plagiarists Profit from Self-Published Ebooks

Self-publishing has become the latest vehicle for spammers and content farms, with the sheer volume of self-published books making it difficult, if not impossible, for e-stores like Amazon to vet works before they go on sale.... Writing a book is hard.... It's a whole lot easier to copy and paste someone else's work, slap your name on top, and wait for the money to roll in. This creates a strong economic incentive, with fake authors ... earning 70% royalty rates on every sale, earning far more than a spammer could with click fraud.

Adam L. Penenberg, Fast Company, *January 16, 2012.*

and in terms of after-sales monitoring, Nijmeh states: "We do spot checks, but it's hard to monitor since some of our members use content in a variety of ways." This can lead to duplicate versions of the same content. Reece seems to reflect the same view: "In basic PLR you can generally change all aspects of the copy and apply your pen name to it. You can also go ahead and sell that to people."

McDonald offers a similar view of the problems faced by such an open platform: "While Lulu's mission is to empower anyone to publish anywhere, anytime; there have been instances of plagiarism and copyright violation."

Amazon Makes Infringement Easier

This type of violation was experienced firsthand by SKS Perry who found his book had been taken by another 'author' and was available on Amazon. "I was doing a vanity search of my name on Google when I noticed a page for Amazon.co.uk listing *Darkside* by SKS Perry. When I linked to the page I saw that it was, in fact, my novel for sale."

Perry isn't the only person facing this issue, and TheyStoleMyBook.com lists other authors who have had their work reproduced illegally, often in the case of free books being repackaged at a price. For Perry he reported the book via Amazon, filed a DMCA [Digital Millennium Copyright Act] takedown notice, left phone messages with Amazon and sent additional paperwork before the book was taken down.

Before the book was removed Perry carried out an experiment to see if Amazon would allow another version of the book to be listed by him. He was able to upload exactly the same content and create a duplicate version of the book on the site. What really surprised Perry is that his book was "under review" before it was made live for 48 hours, but was still allowed through the process, despite being identical to another existing book on the Amazon database.

When the book was removed Perry received neither confirmation nor any compensation for sales that occurred from the fake version of his book. He was never given any indication that the author of the fake version had been punished in any way, other than the book being removed. No information was detailed on actions that would stop the fake author repeating the process in the future.

Not All PLR Content Is Created Equal

While Amazon, Lulu and Smashwords all offer options to report bad content, the onus is on writers to find their stolen content in the first place. Coker suggests running Google searches for strings of content from an author's book as a means of seeing if it has been reproduced elsewhere. All three providers emphasise that they have automated and manual checks in place to spot bad content, but as shown by Perry these are not always effective.

While Reece and Nijmeh create original content, they both admit that many PLR sellers have terrible mass-produced text. "I think some people get very lazy with PLR and don't want to change any elements of it so what happens is you get terrible duplicates," explains Reece, pointing out that even with a good team of writers, "it's important to note that what the buyer does with the PLR is up to them."

A Three-Point Defence System

So does customer protection instead lie with ebook content providers? One line of defence Coker highlights is a three-point system, with Smashwords relying on its filters and the community to spot problems, and that Smashwords itself acts as judge and jury, taking all claims of copyright violation seriously. For Lulu the only automated check is to look at whether an ISBN has been used before, something that can quickly be bypassed with a fake ISBN, with other checks occurring manually when a 'report this content' button is clicked on any book.

Both McDonald and Coker stress that any questionable content will result in a ban for the author. Unless they can prove ownership, the authors will lose any accrued revenue from the current quarter. This gives them three months to find stolen content, which compared to a shorter payment system for Amazon allows for a much higher chance of catching bad content before any money is lost.

None of this completely stops the issue of poor-quality PLR content, which could simply be of low quality or have no formatting for ebooks. In this case another line of defence is implemented by Lulu and Smashwords, at the request of the platforms to which they distribute, including Apple and Barnes & Noble. McDonald puts it best: "As Lulu continues to grow our global network of third-party retailers; we must adhere to their guidelines to ensure the utmost quality for our authors' content and their customers."

Content Guidelines Impact Quality

This level of regulation is driven by Apple which insists on a six-week turnaround for all books and apps. Smashwords and Lulu have to ensure the content they provide to Apple is of high quality, or they risk losing these distribution agreements. When Coker first signed a distribution deal with Barnes & Noble he introduced a "premium catalogue" to only provide them with the best books. Over time this evolved in to a 60-page style guide which all books submitted to these high end sites via Smashwords must abide by. An automatic tool then checks books against these guidelines, and a manual check is made on every book before it is sent. Lulu also uses ePub validation guidelines to ensure formatting for high-end sites is correct before they will accept a book.

All of these checks are great for Apple, but are not enforced by Amazon whose 48-hour turnarounds has seen them accused of duplicate books and poor-quality content. Coker is not convinced Amazon is as effective as it could be: "We have deleted the accounts of dozens of PLR scammers, and often I'll see those same scammers turn around and upload their content directly to Amazon. The Kindle Store is awash in it." He continues: "They aggregate a larger customer audience, and they let a lot of stolen stuff through."

Amazon did not respond to repeated requests for comment over a number of weeks.

Diminishing Customers' Experiences

One such tool is designed to manipulate the system by re-packaging public domain content scraped from the web in to quick ebooks. Owners of the software can generate hundreds of books and it promises "totally hands-free income."

None of this is good for consumers, and as Coker puts it, "The risk of PLR is that you see 50 copies of the same book on the same shelf written by equally lazy-ass idiots who got suckered in to the scam. Then customers, trusting they're buying a real book, purchase these books of questionable value."

Digital books are still at the early part of their life cycle and many customers are embracing the ebook format for the first time. Impulse purchases that result in low-quality content are not likely to lead to future sales for legitimate authors. Likewise any books which are purchased legitimately but found to be stolen by another author will be removed from a customer's device through no fault of their own.

The Fight Continues

Although both McDonald and Coker are quick to highlight that they have only seen a small percentage of authors affected they agree that more can be done. For Coker and Smashwords it is about control and punishment: "I think we make the PLR folks jump through more hoops, our vetting is tighter and more effective, and we simply make it more difficult for them to earn a dime off the scams." McDonald and Lulu are focused on the legal aspect of PLR and stolen content: "We must stay on top of all laws or make a blanket decision to not distribute public domain content outside of the US."

Even with these systems in place, Coker feels that "ebooks will continue to attract the dregs of the cybercrime underworld." While PLR can contain well-researched content, it is also being manipulated on a grand scale both by people who write poor-quality content, or buyers who repackage the same content in multiple ways. Ultimately while the main providers of ebooks are taking action and giving customers and authors the power to take back control there are clear loopholes that need to be closed.

"There's a whole spectrum of grey areas ... [where] it's not clear ... that [appropriating online text] is either equivalent to theft or copyright infringement because the analogy to real property doesn't fully hold."

Copyright Infringement of E-books Is an Ethical Grey Area

Martin Paul Eve

Martin Paul Eve is a lecturer in English literature at the University of Lincoln in Great Britain. In the following viewpoint, Eve takes on the ethical grey area of e-book infringement. Drawing on an actual incident of infringement, Eve discusses the legal differences between copyright infringement and theft and how consumers are having difficulty assessing the value of digital products because they do not receive a physical, material object in exchange for their money. Publishers, meanwhile, are trying to simultaneously make their e-books a commodity—something that has value from purchasing its physical form—and licensed content—something the consumer has only paid to use and does not own—Eve writes. According to the author, Amazon is the worst offender, overcharging for content and stripping consumers of all rights and artists of their fair share of the profit. The shakedown in digital publishing commodities is far from settled, Eve concludes.

As you read, consider the following questions:

1. What Marxist idea does Eve use in his argument against materialism?

2. According to Eve, what does Richard Stallman say is the problem with intellectual property?

3. What ethical problems are raised by Amazon's e-book publishing arm, according to the author?

Last night, as I was heading to bed, a guy called Mark Ko-hut, whom I know from various [author Thomas] Pynchon-interest intersections, published a copy of a letter he was planning to send to the *New York Times*. The contention turned over a column on the *NYT*'s website called Pogue's posts in which David Pogue stated that he had downloaded a copy of "The Bourne Identity" e-book, knowing it was unauthorised (having failed to find an e-copy legitimately: which, by the way, is total rubbish), and had sent a cheque for $9.99 to "the publisher" instead. I want to write about a few of the issues here as I tweeted Mark back with a statement that conflating copyright violation with theft is actually incorrect. I then deleted the tweet as I was going to bed and realised that it might just be over-inflammatory. That said, Mark saw it and responded (graciously). I agree with Mark that Pogue's broadcast of this availability is problematic, but I also think it's worth reasoning through some of the unspoken assumptions of the model here. Before I begin, I want to stress that all examples in this post are purely hypothetical; thought experiments designed to expose the tangled relations in the current setup. I buy all my books.

E-book Digital Rights Management May Push People to Piracy

Platforms age and die. This summer, Microsoft is turning off the DRM [digital rights management] servers for Microsoft Reader. This means that people who bought Microsoft Reader e-books over the decade since 2002 now find that their e-books are trapped inside a rapidly ageing, obsolescent slab of plastic and glass. In another 5–10 years, 95% of those books will be unreadable because the machines they're locked into were designed by a CE [consumer electronics] industry obsessed with the 2–3 year upgrade cycle—they're not durable. This is actually one psychological driver for piracy—people who have paid for a book resent being expected to pay for it again due to an arbitrary-seeming lock-in onto an aging piece of hardware. From their point of view, honesty is being punished.

There is no guarantee that B&N [Barnes and Noble] will stay in business, or that Amazon won't discontinue support for older Kindle files, in the not too distant future.

Charlie Stross, Charlie's Diary *(blog),*
April 24, 2012. www.antipope.org.

Consumers Fail to See the Artist's Labor

A basic moral precept/starting proposition to begin. If you disagree with this, the logic from here on may also seem flawed: We live in a (neoliberal) capitalist world. Under that system, which is far from perfect, artists, writers, publishers and all involved in the publication process should be compensated for their work (ideally, I'd like this done through arts programmes, rather than selling their work, but that's a different story). Many artforms seem more vulnerable than most products, though, to being seen as commodity fetishes. Commodity fetishism is [nineteenth-century socialist philosopher Karl] Marx's term under which, instead of seeing the social relations, we see only the material relations; we see things, not people. In this instance, we see a CD or a slim book and feel that, instead of paying for the artist's labour, we are paying for the item which is, in itself, cheap to produce. In the twentieth century, before electronic books and music, it was necessary to have a physical medium present to read each book or play back recorded music. This was bad enough for commodity fetishism, but now that we have the electronic form only, many believe that as there is no cost associated with the production of the material item (there is no material item), there should be no cost in its acquisition. This is a flawed argument, as I'll go on to show, but there are also flaws on the other side as well.

Copyright Infringement Is Not Theft

Copyright infringement is the unauthorised sharing (not receiving) of somebody else's "intellectual property". As Richard Stallman, outspoken founder of the CopyLeft movement, sees it, however, this term "intellectual property" is problematic: "it suggests thinking about copyright, patents and trademarks by analogy with property rights for physical objects". In Stallman's view, one of the problems is that this term conflates three very separate areas of law (copyright/patents/trademarks) with different functions into one crude analogy. When thought of as "intellectual property", copyright violation becomes analogous to theft. In law, however, it isn't. Copyright violation is a civil suit: you have caused injury to a party and may be called upon to provide redress that will be enforced by the legal framework. Theft, on the other hand, is a criminal matter that can be dealt with by imprisonment. The difference between the forms rests on deprivation of tangible property that occurs in theft, as opposed to only potential deprivation in copyright on a probabilistic basis that can never be fully demonstrated.

Some Hypothetical Examples

To explain this, consider theft and copyright infringement in various hypothetical circumstances. If I take a material object of yours, I have gained that object at your cost; you no longer have it. Conversely, let's say that you are selling your music and I copy one of your CDs. You still have the original CD. I have a copy of the music on the CD. What has been lost is not the material item, but the future potential for you to sell the product of your labour to me. The equivalence between future potential earnings and theft cannot be a one-to-one ratio, though: there is no guarantee that I would have bought your CD in the first place. In this instance, there has been no material disadvantage to you. At the other extreme, if I copied your CD so that I didn't have to buy it, then the loss to you, mediated through finance, is almost identical to theft. There's a whole spectrum of grey areas in between when we work with this artificial model: lending CDs to friends, buying one copy of the CD for an entire household, the instance when downloading prompts someone to buy something they wouldn't have otherwise, etc. and it's not clear, in many of these, that it is either equivalent to theft or copyright infringement because the analogy to real property doesn't fully hold.

Space-Shifting Is Not Theft

So far, so good. Now let's consider this particular case. Downloading a product (that doesn't exist in retail form), the content of which is identical to a product that does exist in retail form, and paying the cost of the retail form. I agree with Mark that there is the potential here that the money has gone to the wrong people. I'm definitely sure that I think, differently to Mark, that this is different to theft. In fact, this is a mightily strange one.

If publishers want to take the human-relations side of the commodity fetish coin (the product is more than its materiality), then the price for which they are selling the material entity should cover, by their projections, labour + the cost of materials/transport etc. How then is the labour component of this purchase, the literature within, different to the virtualised form? I'm not sure it is. Let's say, as another hypothetical argument, that I have bought a physical copy of a book and I then decide, for my own personal use only, to type the contents of that book, word for word into my computer and then re-package it in e-book format for my e-reader (again for my own use only). Is this equivalent, morally, to theft? I don't think so (in fact, I've surely paid over the odds for the virtual version as I paid for the additional material costs on top of the human-relations costs), but many publishers think so and now include licensing terms in the front of their books thus:

> No part of this publication may be reproduced, stored in a retrieval system, or transmitted, in any form or by any means, without the prior permission of the publisher

This means that, in essence, publishers are trying to have their cake and eat it. They want to consider materiality and social relations as intertwined, even in the case where there is no material object. As far as I can see, the book in question in this particular case does not come with this legal licensing requirement, in at least two of the prints I checked.

Amazon Monopolises the E-book Market

There are further ethical problems with the e-book market that should also be taken into consideration. This ethical problem is called: Amazon. Amazon pays, in the UK, no corporation tax. Yet it is putting many booksellers completely out of business, forcing independent artists to sell their art at a far cheaper rate than is viable, and monopolising the e-book market via Kindle's lock-in while taking vast chunks of the profit. I refuse to condone Amazon's behaviour and, while they behave in this way, it seems to me that it would be far less of a moral compromise to pirate an e-book and pay for the material version, direct (albeit with my already stated wariness, alongside Mark, about where the money goes), than it would have been to have bought the paperback from Amazon. Even better, buy a paperback copy from a high street [a British commercial area] retailer (preferably a small, independent).

To conclude, as I've gone on long enough (even though only scratching the surface): I think, in ethical (rather than purely legal) terms, the debate here is far more complex than a straight comparison to theft. At the same time, I appreciate exactly where Mark is coming from: publishers are here caught in the middle and being blamed for things that aren't their fault. The only way that I think this can be resolved is through a protracted discussion of exactly *what*, is being sold in the case of a material book vs. an e-book, *how* that relates to commodity fetishism and *what* can be done to ensure the continued viability of bookselling and publishing, in material and virtual forms, when monopolies like Amazon are creating huge problems both financially and ethically.

> *"Can copyright adapt itself to the digital age? . . . The answer . . . is a resounding 'yes.'"*

Copyright Policy Can Adapt to Changing Technology

Laurence Kaye

Laurence Kaye is a lawyer specializing in intellectual property, media, and digital law. In the following viewpoint, Kaye discusses the changing field of copyright law in the United Kingdom. He writes that although some perceive copyright as irrelevant in the digital era, in fact copyright law is crucial to protecting the copyright of digital intellectual property. However, he asserts, the differences in technology necessitate changes in copyright law to close loopholes and broaden fair uses. For example, Kaye explains, the problem of orphan works (where the copyright holder is indeterminable or uncontactable) needs to be legislated, and educators need clarification of fair use of digital materials to use in their classrooms. Kaye is confident that the changes the UK government makes to copyright law will bring clarity to the muddle of how copyright intersects with digital technology.

As you read, consider the following questions:

1. Why does Kaye argue that there is no copyright in ideas?

2. According to Kaye, what five elements are significant for copyright's adaptation to the digital era?

3. What copyright exception is the UK government considering for libraries, according to the author?

Copyright works, created by professionals and amateurs alike, are ubiquitous [everywhere] on the network, on social media platforms, websites and online services. In June this year [2012], the Intellectual Property Office (IPO) and Imperial College published new estimates of investment in the UK's copyright industries, of which the publishing industry is a significant part. When adopted in the National Accounts this adds more than £3 billion to the economy.

Yet at the same time, copyright faces a tidal pressure for change. It is often portrayed as a negative force, a hindrance to the economy and as a drag on growth. More fundamentally, many critics say that the internet, digital technology and social media are turning copyright into an anachronism.

Copyright Is Integral to the Economy

This is not an academic debate. Copyright is at the heart of the digital publishing industry. In place of the sale of a book as a physical product, the digital transaction is the grant of a licence to access, stream, rent, download to own, share and to use creative content in an ever increasing variety of ways. So copyright is truly at the heart of publisher's digital business models, even if challenges remain around pricing, illegal copying via peer-to-peer file sharing networks and the consumer's willingness to pay. Publishers therefore have a vested interest in the policy and practical solutions which are needed to ensure that copyright truly becomes, and is seen as, an enabler of the digital economy.

In truth, this is not really a paradox. Copyright cannot be heading for extinction and at the same time underpin the digital economy. This apparent contradiction is a product of the "digital shift". It reflects differing perspectives on copyright and an on-going process of adaptation of law, policy, business models and the way technology is used to make copyright function more efficiently online.

Copyright Is Not a Barrier

There are two features of the digital shift that have made these differences in perspective more acute. The first is sometimes dressed in the language of freedom of expression on the internet but is essentially a consequence of the desire for mass digitisation and the mass use of copyright works. Copyright is a permissions-based system and for that reason copyright can, wrongly in my view, be portrayed as a barrier.

The second relates to the shift of copyright from business-to-business to business-to-consumer in the online world. Copyright law is complex but the consumer is shielded from this complexity in the physical world where the transaction is the purchase of a book, a physical good. Not so in the digital world where everyone is in the B2C business, from publishers and authors as self-publishers to e-tailers such as Amazon and Apple and to consumers. The consumer/reader, whether or not they bother to read the terms and conditions, are licence-holders and, as such, buyers of copyright rights.

So can copyright adapt itself to the digital age? Can a system built on a collection of national copyrights function adequately in an internet-enabled world where national boundaries are crossed at a click? Can it provide an effective mechanism to incentivise, reward and protect creators and producers of works whilst at the same time enabling access to that wealth of creativity?

The answer to all these questions is a resounding "yes". Copyright is a Darwinian species but it needs to continue to evolve to meet the needs of today's always-on networked society.

Copyright Is Format Neutral

There are three fundamental reasons why copyright has the inherent capacity to adapt.

When Mozart or Beethoven composed an entire work in their head, it became a copyright work before it was ever recorded on paper as a musical composition. It's true that national copyright laws require the work to be recorded in some medium, either analogue or digital, before the work qualifies for protection under copyright law. But that doesn't alter the fact that the work is still a copyright work in its immaterial form. To turn [1960s social scientist] Marshall McLuhan's dictum on its head, it's the message, not the medium.

We are beginning to see a shift in focus away from the book to a "format-neutral" version of the narrative or story. One of the opportunities in the digital age is to take the world embodied in the story and to extend aspects of it across multiple platforms in ways which play to the strengths of each of those platforms and which tell different parts of those stories in fresh and engaging ways. This is the approach which underlies "transmedia" or "cross-media". As Jeff Gomez (CEO, Starlight Runner Entertainment), transmedia guru, puts it, "For publishers it offers the opportunity to participate in revenue streams from every way in which the property is monetised."

Telling stories across platforms is not a universal panacea for all works, and it may involve significant investment. But as [journalist] Benedicte Page pointed out in *The Bookseller*, "Publishers must explore transmedia approaches to engage children whose lives revolve increasingly around gaming, online communities and social networking."

However, it's high time that the focus switched to the role of copyright licensing to drive business. As one publisher put it at the Futurebook event this year, "I've told my staff to stop talking about *selling books* and start talking about *licensing a copyright*."

There Is No Copyright in Ideas

There is a misconception that copyright gives a monopoly over ideas. It doesn't. Copyright is often portrayed as an obstacle or barrier to the way new works are created in the digital age, standing as a King Canute [an early king of England] against a tide of mash-ups. But that misses the key point about copyright.

Ideas are a freely exchangeable currency on the internet. Lawyers talk about the "idea/expression" dichotomy. Put simply, copyright does not protect ideas, but only what the courts now call "the author's own intellectual creation" which is reflected in the way those ideas are expressed.

In a recent decision by the European Court of Justice (*SAS Institute Inc. v. World Programming Ltd* (C-406/10)), it was decided that the ideas and functionality of a computer program cannot be protected by copyright, so there is no infringement unless the source code is copied.

UK copyright law, in line with the continental European approach, increasingly talks about copyright protecting only the "author's own intellectual creation". So if someone finds their own way of expressing the ideas embodied in a work, without copying the work itself, they are free to do so.

Even where copying takes place, there is no infringement unless the whole or a substantial part is taken. So, generally speaking, taking small parts of a work on an irregular basis is not restricted by copyright law.

Checks and Balances Are Built In

The role of copyright law has always been to balance the rights given to authors, performers and producers to incentivise and reward their creations with the public interest to have access to those works. The levers which maintain this balance in copyright law are copyright exceptions and legal constraints which derive from competition law and the concept of free movement of goods and services.

There are extensive exceptions built into copyright legislation which allow copyright works to be used without permission for purposes such as education, research and private study, reporting current events, criticism and review. Some of those exceptions need updating and, following the Hargreaves Review, a number of changes are in the legal pipeline.

Competition law, and the rules in Europe governing the free movement of goods and services, also play a restraining influence in the way copyright is exercised, especially in the area of territorial licensing. For instance, the European Court of Justice recently decided (in *UsedSoft GmbH v. Oracle International Corp*, Case C-128/11, 3 July 2012.), that once a lawfully acquired and paid-for copy of a software product has been downloaded from the internet, which included a licence to use the copy for consideration for an unlimited period of time, the software owner could not prevent the re-sale of that copy. In legal speak, the software owner's distribution right under copyright was "exhausted".

Contractual Restrictions

Another important case focused on contractual restrictions. In 2010, actions were brought in the High Court in two cases involving pubs that bought cheap foreign satellite-decoder equipment and cards for use in screening live football matches in UK pubs, so as to avoid the higher fees charged by the satellite broadcast rights-holder in the UK. In one case, the Football Association Premiere League (FAPL) sought to prevent the circumvention of the exclusive territorial licences and brought actions against Greek suppliers of equipment and decoders into pubs and against the licensees of four pubs that showed live Premier League matches broadcast on the channels of an Arab broadcaster. The second case stemmed from an appeal against conviction in criminal proceedings brought against Karen Murphy, the landlady of a pub who showed Premier League matches using a Greek decoder card.

The cases were referred to the Advocate General of the European Court of Justice. He concluded that a contractual obligation, linked to a broadcasting licence, requiring the broadcaster to prevent its satellite decoder cards from being used outside the licensed territory, is equivalent to an agreement to prevent or restrict parallel exports. Such licences with absolute territorial protection are incompatible with the internal market and breach Article 101(1) of the TFEU [Treaties on the Functioning of the European Union], without it being necessary to show the actual effect on competition. The Advocate General also concluded that the licences breach the freedom to provide services in Article 59 of the TFEU, without legitimate justification.

Five Elements of Adaptation

There is no "silver bullet". I would suggest there are five interrelated elements in copyright's adaptation to the digital age: the law, technology, business models, education and enforcement.

Here I cover changes in copyright law; for the other elements do request the full white paper.

There is work to be done in the law at an international as well as a national level. There are still some legal questions to answer such as when a work is made available on the network, does this take place at the point of upload, download or both? The relevance is in knowing where to clear the rights. This is a question before the European Court of Justice at the moment.

At a national level, change to UK copyright law is fairly imminent. Following the publication of the *Hargreaves Review* ("Digital Opportunity, A Review of Intellectual Property and Growth") in May 2011, the Government published a Consultation on Copyright in December 2011 on a number of quite far-reaching changes to UK copyright law and in June it published a summary of the responses it received to the Consultation.

Many of the possible changes on which the Government consulted have been under discussion for a number of years, following periodic reviews including the Gower Review in 2005. But it now looks as though we are actually going to see some change. How far reaching the changes will be is difficult to say at the time of writing this report, because the Government has not yet made its intentions public. But the Government is looking for a quick route to introduce a number of changes to copyright exceptions under secondary legislation enabled by the Enterprise and Regulatory Reform Bill.

Two Broad Categories of Changes

The proposed changes fall into two broad categories broadening or updating existing exceptions to copyright law and introducing statutory licensing solutions in two areas "orphan works" and "extended collective licensing".

There are several proposed changes where there is consensus between copyright stakeholders. For instance, almost everyone supports a solution to the problem of orphan works, i.e., copyright works whose owner is unknown. The likely solution will involve a requirement to carry out a "diligent search" to try and find that owner and, if they cannot be found, getting a licence from a collecting society to permit non-commercial use (and, possibly, commercial use as well) of the orphan work with provision for remuneration being paid to the owner if and when they appear.

Also, in the field of copyright exceptions, there is general agreement that it makes sense to extend the existing exception which allows libraries and archives to make copies of literary and artistic works for digital preservation to cover sound recordings, films and broadcasts as well. In the educational field, it is logical to extend the current exception which allows teachers and examiners to make "chalk and talk" copies of work to enable them to use digital white boards.

Space-Shifting Is Being Debated

So updating certain exceptions to reflect the realities of the digital world makes sense. But there will be conflict between rights-holders and users where exceptions could potentially undermine licence-based business models or deprive rights owners of remuneration to which they may otherwise be entitled.

As I have already observed, in the world of digital media, the transaction between the supplier and the consumer is licence-based. So removing the need for licensing by broadening or introducing an exception which could have a commercial impact is a real and legitimate concern for rights-holders.

Here is one example. The Government is considering a private copying exception to allow consumers to copy a lawfully acquired work from one format to another. Of course, the record industry has tolerated this for years and many online services allow consumers to have a number of copies of the same work on different devices. But, as in all things, the devil is in the detail. Many rights-holders are worried that it could adversely impact on already declining revenues, pointing to the fact that elsewhere in Europe rights-holders are compensated for private copying by equipment and other forms of levies. The UK Government is not intending to introduce a levy scheme for private copying in the UK. But some rights-holders are worried. For instance, if private copies held on "cloud-based" services were permitted under an exception, could that have a commercial impact?

The Exception for Data Mining

Another controversial exception is for text and data mining, defined in the *Hargreaves Review* as "the automated analytical techniques such as text and data mining work by copying existing electronic information, for instance articles in scientific journals and other works, and analysing the data they contain for patterns, trends and other useful information". Whilst it is common ground amongst all stakeholders that there is no copyright in facts, there is industry concern that a copyright exception for content mining could prejudice the primary market for, or value of, the copyright works. The industry would certainly prefer to facilitate data mining by licensing solutions and not by a copyright exception.

> *"Advancing technology is rapidly making enforcement of traditional copyright-dependent business models essentially impossible."*

Changing Technology Has Made Traditional Copyright Policy Obsolete

Chad Perrin

Chad Perrin is an information technology consultant and a writer. In the following viewpoint, Perrin discusses the changing face of business in the copyright industry. Neither a liberal nor a conservative reading of copyright law and its enforcement can bridge the gaps opening up in light of changing digital technology, the author maintains. Perrin argues that copyright enforcement is becoming obsolete and that traditional copyright industries must adapt or be pushed out. Because copying content has become so inexpensive and easy for both consumers and businesses it makes no sense to form a business model that relies on scarcity, Perrin writes. Businesses that can find a way to provide content and make money without concerning themselves with piracy, concludes the author, are those best poised for survival, if not success, in the digital era.

As you read, consider the following questions:

1. What are the two factions of copyright enforcement, according to the author?

2. According to Perrin, how has mass production changed since the advent of digital technology?

3. Why does Perrin argue that preventing people from making copies of copyrighted works is a waste of time and money?

The ongoing controversies over matters of copyright enforcement and piracy are infected by virulent strains of propaganda and misunderstanding. The entire issue is commonly framed as a battle between content creators and peer-to-peer file sharers. Let us take the two most extreme views, and refer to them by names they often choose for themselves. At one extreme, there are the defenders of "content owners" who either believe that copyright is a basic property right imperfectly embodied in law or who just believe that treating copyright that way is an important expedient that they should defend. At the other extreme, there are the "copyfighters" who believe that copyright is an authoritarian imposition, establishing harmful monopolies, either as corrupt and immoral support for capitalist plutocrats, or as unconscionable governmental interference in markets that should be free.

The Two Extremes
Spread Misunderstanding

The copyfighter faction favors serving the consumer, often whether a given consumer has paid for what he or she consumes or not; strong protections provided by the legal doctrine of "fair use"; and free peer to peer file sharing. They sometimes characterize their counterparts as nothing more than corrupt politicians and fatcat corporate bureaucrats making obscene amounts of money doing nothing but taking egregious advantage of the financial and legal vulnerability of both actual content creators and content consumers.

The content owner faction favors strict copyright enforcement including DRM, draconian legal penalties for copyright infringement (or even any act that could conceivably look like infringement or accidentally contribute to it), and other measures that sometimes get on the EFF's [Electronic Frontier Foundation's] bad side. This faction typically portrays file sharers as conscienceless thieves who just want to get something for nothing. Anyone who consistently enough argues against DRM [digital rights management] and six-figure penalties for file sharing in online discussion eventually gets accused of stealing, and using their arguments against strict copyright enforcement for no purpose other than to excuse that behavior—regardless of whether they actually engage in any infringing file sharing at all.

Like most issues normally cast in black and white terms, the reality is much more complex than that, and these two extremes lie at opposite ends of a spectrum of opinion, with most people falling somewhere along that spectrum other than the ends. As with most such oversimplifications, a reasonable, best truth for almost any useful definitions of "best" and "truth" will involve some basic principles poached from both ends, filling in the gaps with common sense. While I have my own ideas of what is best, easily discovered to some degree by following me around in TechRepublic discussions for a little while, sharing those ideas in general is not the purpose of this article.

Traditional Industries Must Change

Regardless of your personal beliefs about what *should* be the state of copyright law, the reality is that advancing technology is rapidly making enforcement of traditional copyright-dependent business models essentially impossible. Old-school media organizations are facing the problem of trying to figure

Public Goods Are Difficult to Regulate

For traditional copyright lawyers, the transformation of copyright law in the public's perception—from noble curator of the springs of creativity to, as in [Harvard] professor [Charles] Nesson's view, a "contaminant" that vexes the lives of free people—has been dizzying.

By enabling the nearly costless distribution of perfect copies of music, books, and movies, digital technologies intensified a behavioral enigma that always lay at the heart of copyright law. These works are what economists call public goods. Once someone publicly sings a song, it's impossible to keep others from singing it, and the fact that they will won't prevent the songwriter from continuing to sing his song. Thomas Jefferson famously captured these intoxicating facets of public goods more memorably than anyone else: "He who receives an idea from me, receives instruction himself without lessening mine; as he who lights his taper at mine, receives light without darkening me."

Roger Parloff, Fortune, *July 11, 2012.*

out how they can change their business models to stay in the game, with the inherent problem of being built around their old models, unwilling to abandon those old models entirely, and lacking the ability to substantively change those models without replacing most of their workforces and losing decades of both expertise and brand trust. Meanwhile, media prices are often perceived as unreasonably high, the old models in many ways are far less convenient for the consumer than piracy-driven media distribution regardless of price, and the cost of using the law and inherently flawed technological measures to fight piracy is spiralling out of control as network technologies improve at an accelerating rate.

Easy Mass Production Drives Change

Much of the current state of affairs is a direct result of the fact that powerful media distributors have grown comfortable with a very profitable business model that is rapidly becoming obsolete. That model is predicated upon assumptions developed during a time when the tools of mass production were prohibitively expensive and mass distribution cost even more. Today, mass production is a trivially employed side-effect of the way computers—including computers some people in barely industrialized countries carry around in their pockets—work on their most fundamental level, while mass distribution is almost automatic for computers attached to the Internet. As their assumptions are challenged by the increasing ease of copying and distributing content, the business interests invested in revenue models built on those assumptions are doing what they can to undermine and forestall the effects of those challenges.

Fighting an Uphill Battle

Over time, the vested interests that support strict copyright enforcement have been fighting an uphill battle against inevitable technological advancement. As desperation grows, so does the extremity to which the desperate are willing to take their efforts. Their tactics involve attacking the doctrine of fair use, expanding the reach of copyright law, the abuse of patent law, and intensive propaganda campaigns. The result has for the most part been that those products placed in the vanguard of strict copyright enforcement end up the most-pirated or the least-purchased.

Part of the propagandizing that goes on involves inventing new terms, or misapplying old terms, to confuse the nature of copyright law in the minds of the general public. By calling copyrightable and patentable materials "intellectual property", for instance, there is a strong correlation drawn between copyright infringement and theft where no such correlation exists by nature. Contrary to the implications of terms like "intellectual property", copyright is not a matter of property law: it is a government enforced monopoly on the manufacture and distribution of copies of a particular work. The key difference lies in the fact that in the case of copyright infringement a copy is made of the original without permission, while in the case of theft the original is actually removed from its possessor. This difference is recognized in law, in the communications of the founders and constitutional framers of the United States, and in everyday life.

Removal of property from its possessor is a definitive requirement of the term "theft". As the *Merriam-Webster* dictionary defines theft:

> the act of stealing; specifically: the felonious taking and removing of personal property with intent to deprive the rightful owner of it.

Preventing Theft Is Easy

Note the term *removing*. In case that is not clear enough, consider this visual guide, distributed under the terms of the Creative Commons BY-ND License:

The reason copyright infringement is so difficult to prevent under traditional copyright-dependent business models is quite simply that the aim of preventing such infringement involves trying to keep people from making copies of what you have already given them. Preventing theft is (relatively speaking) easy; just keep your doors locked and theft becomes an extreme rarity, because you possess something and want to stop someone else from getting it. Preventing copyright infringement is another can of worms entirely, because enforcement then consists of convincing the person who possesses something to refrain from doing things with it in the comfort and privacy of his or her own home.

People May and Will Make Copies

The advancement of technology, so far, has only served to strengthen our ability to prevent people from removing things from our homes without our permission, but at the same time the advancement of technology has only served to strengthen our ability to make copies of copyrightable content as well, and technology is not getting any less advanced. To complicate matters for distributors in copyright dependent industries, the increasing ease and decreasing cost of copying content is actually a tremendous boon to those distributors' bottom lines, because as it gets cheaper to copy content, the profit margin for each copy sold gets bigger.

Regardless of your feelings about the matter of whether copyright enforcement is justified, it makes little sense to cover our ears, close our eyes, and ignore the facts that face us. In the end, if you want to make money by providing content for others' consumption in years to come, you are going to have to start recognizing the increasing difficulty of maintaining a state of artificial scarcity enforced by copyright law. The most successful media distributors will be those who can employ a business model that does not assume users can be prevented from making copies. Give people positive reinforcement for not making copies as an inherent feature of the model or, better yet, employ a model that relies on the natural tendency people have to share what what they like when it is essentially free to copy.

A Waste of Time and Money

The opposite approach—assuming people cannot make copies at home, followed by trying to force that state of affairs on customers—is a great way to burn incredible sums of money in a futile effort to counteract the advancement of technology that in many ways actually helps your own business model. Even if you think customers making copies of what you have sold is immoral, taking the position that this means the traditional business models reliant on strict copyright enforcement are not rapidly and irresistibly disintegrating around us is quickly taking on the character of an astonishing act of stupidity.

Strict copyright enforcement is not quite obsolete yet, but obsolescence is definitely nipping at its heels. If your plans for a copyright dependent business model do not include a way to transition to a model that does not rely on strict copyright enforcement, you are not really practicing business for the long term; you are just engaging in short-sighted, willful ignorance. The only way to secure your content-based business model for the future is to find a way to make money without treating copyrightable works as property that can be secured.

Periodical and Internet Sources Bibliography

The following articles have been selected to supplement the diverse viewpoints presented in this chapter.

Michael A. Carrier	"Copyright and Innovation: The Untold Story," *Wisconsin Law Review*, 2012.
Devin Coldewey	"10-Year-Old Girl's Laptop Confiscated After Copyright Offense," NBC News, November 27, 2013. www.nbcnews.com.
Tim Cushing	"Japanese Government to Start Seeding P2P Networks with Faux Files Containing Copyright Warnings," *Techdirt* (blog), February 5, 2013. www.techdirt.com.
Josh Halliday	"Unauthorized TV Live Streaming Breaches Copyright, Rules European Copyright," *The Guardian* (Manchester, UK), March 7, 2013. www.guardian.co.uk.
Garrett McCord	"Theft of a Food Blog: Copyright Infringement in the E-book Marketplace," *Huffington Post*, August 3, 2012. www.huffingtonpost.com.
Ms. Smith	"P2P Blocklists Fail to Protect Privacy from Copyright Cops' Mass Monitoring," *NetworkWorld*, September 5, 2012. www.networkworld.com.
Joanna Stern	"Starting Today, It's Illegal to Unlock Your Cellphones," ABC News, January 26, 2013. http://abcnews.go.com.
Hayley Tsukayama	"The Circuit: YouTube Loses Copyright Battle, Bill Shock, Sprint Nextel," *Washington Post*, April 20, 2012.
United States Department of Justice	"Federal Courts Order Seizure of Three Website Domains Involved in Distributing Pirated Android Cell Phone Apps," August 21, 2012. www.justice.gov.

For Further Discussion

Chapter 1

1. What crucial assumption does Jonathan Pink make to support his argument of copyright infringement as theft? Do you agree with him? Why or why not? Ben Jones does not agree with Pink and outlines the differences between civil and criminal lawsuits to make his point. Do you find Jones's viewpoint more or less compelling than Pink's. Why?

2. Using the viewpoints by Martin Ammori and Corynne McSherry to inform your answer, explain whether you think the sale of used digital goods constitutes copyright infringement or whether it should fall under the umbrella of first-sale doctrine, as other used goods do, like books and CDs. Do you think first-sale doctrine is worth preserving, or does it harm the economy? Explain.

Chapter 2

1. After reading the viewpoints by the Department of Professional Employees (DPE) and Julian Sanchez, do you believe that copyright infringement is having a negative effect on the economy? What are the strongest arguments in favor of each view, and with which viewpoint do you agree? Why?

2. Do you agree with Eriq Gardner that copyright infringement lawsuits create a financial and legal burden on society? Why or why not? Righthaven may have fallen, but other legal firms, like the US Copyright Group, are performing a similar service. Do you think mass lawsuits help to curb infringement, or do they make copyright infringement seem like a bigger problem than it may actually be? Explain.

Chapter 3

1. After reading the viewpoints by Jeffrey D. Neuburger and Fred von Lohmann, do you think the Digital Millennium Copyright Act (DMCA) has been helpful in protecting copyright or does it suppress innovation? Why or why not? If you could make one change to the DMCA to improve its usefulness to society, what would that change be?

2. Do you believe that the Copyright Alert System, which went into effect in February 2013, will curb online infringement, or will it only slow the infringers down? Why? Do you agree with Joey LeMay that the Copyright Alert System violates consumers' rights, or do you think he is overreacting? Explain?

3. After reading the viewpoint by Reihan Salam and Patrick Ruffini, do you think the changes to copyright law since 1978 have had a negative impact on creativity and innovation? Why or why not? Salam and Ruffini believe that the Internet will change how the American economy works. What changes have you observed already? Do you believe these changes support innovation? Why or why not?

Chapter 4

1. Peer-to-peer (P2P) services have arguably been one of the most contentious elements of digital technology since the Napster case in the 1990s. After reading the viewpoints by Kollin J. Zimmermann and Devindra Hardawar, do you think P2P does more harm than good? Why? Case law currently supports the "actual transfer" theory of copyright infringement on P2P services, but Zimmermann argues in favor of the broader "making available" theory. Which theory do you believe applies better, and why?

2. After reading the viewpoints by Mike Essex and Martin Paul Eve, do you think that copyright infringement of e-books is a significant problem? Do you believe a lack of availability contributes to e-book infringement? Explain

your answers. How can self-published authors fight back against those who plagiarize their books?

3. After reading the viewpoints by Laurence Kaye and Chad Perrin, do you believe that current copyright law can effectively serve individuals and business in a digital world? Why or why not? Do you think copyright law needs to change, businesses need to change, both, or neither? Explain your answer, using viewpoints by Kaye and/or Perrin to support your argument.

Organizations to Contact

The editors have compiled the following list of organizations concerned with the issues debated in this book. The descriptions are derived from materials provided by the organizations. All have publications or information available for interested readers. The list was compiled on the date of publication of the present volume; the information provided here may change. Be aware that many organizations take several weeks or longer to respond to inquiries, so allow as much time as possible.

Access Copyright
1 Yonge St., Ste. 800, Toronto, ON   M5E 1E5
  Canada
(416) 868-1620; toll-free: (800) 893-5777 • fax: (416) 868-1621
e-mail: info@accesscopyright.ca
website: www.accesscopyright.ca

Access Copyright is a nonprofit organization that ensures fair compensation for writers, publishers, and artists in Canada by providing a venue through which rights can be licensed and royalties paid. Access Copyright has been providing content to businesses, schools, and government since 1988. It provides publications on its website, including a monthly newsletter, news releases, videos, annual reports, and interviews.

Copyright Clearance Center (CCC)
222 Rosewood Dr., Danvers, MA   01923
(978) 750-8400 • fax: (978) 646-8600
website: www.copyright.com

The Copyright Clearance Center is an organization that specializes in rights and permissions for other organizations, such as academic and commercial publishers. The CCC provides tools and services that help their clients get access to the materials they need, including books, journals, movies, images, blogs, and e-books. Its website provides information about the classes that the CCC offers, as well as the various rights licenses that can be purchased. The CCC has a European subsidiary called RightsDirect.

Creative Commons (CC)
444 Castro St., Suite 900, Mountain View, CA 94041
(650) 294-4732 • fax: (650) 965-1605
website: creativecommons.org

Creative Commons is a nonprofit organization that provides free licenses to people who want to share their work and release some of the rights normally restricted by copyright. CC maintains a symbols standard to make it easy to mark one's work with a CC license and even has an option for those who want to put their work in the public domain. CC provides information and support for those interested in or using CC licenses and links to many projects, organizations, and political bodies who are using a CC license. The website also provides a newsletter, a blog, interviews, and press releases relevant to CC licensing.

Electronic Frontier Foundation (EFF)
815 Eddy St., San Francisco, CA 94109
(415) 436-9333 • fax: (415) 436-9993
e-mail: info@eff.org
website: www.eff.org

The Electronic Frontier Foundation was founded in 1990 to support public interest in privacy, free speech, and innovation. EFF has made itself a force to be reckoned with, sending its lawyers into the courtroom to fight or defend cases that underlie its core value of consumer rights in the realm of technology. On its website are news, white papers, and reports about the cases the EFF is involved in, including a project called Teaching Copyright, which provides a curriculum for educators.

Library Copyright Alliance (LCA)

c/o Association of Research Libraries, Washington, DC   20036
(212) 296-2296
website: www.librarycopyrightalliance.org

The Library Copyright Alliance is a coalition of the American
Library Association, the Association of Research Libraries, and
the Association of College and Research Libraries and was
founded to form a united voice for the three hundred thousand people the LCA represents in matters of copyright law,
including fair use and global access to information. On its
website, the LCA publishes its goals, shares news pertaining to
its mission, and provides records of testimony in Congress
and before the courts.

Library of Congress

101 Independence Ave. SE, Washington, DC   20540
(202) 707-5000
website: www.loc.gov

The Library of Congress is the largest library in the world and
serves as the research arm of the US Congress. The library is a
cultural treasury for the American people, both in its physical
manifestation on Capitol Hill in Washington, DC, and online,
where the Library has made available many free educational
resources and services. Services the library provides include
e-mailing reference questions to the librarians who work there
and asking questions about copyright registration (the US
Copyright Office operates within the jurisdiction of the Library of Congress). On its website, the Library of Congress
has many digital collections of historic materials available, as
well as fully indexed, searchable catalogs for all of the library's
holdings.

Motion Picture Association of America (MPAA)

1600 Eye St. NW, Washington, DC   20006
(202) 293-1966 • fax: (202) 296-7410
website: www.mpaa.org

The Motion Picture Association of America is an advocacy group for the Hollywood film industry, including the six major studios: Disney, Paramount, Sony, Twentieth Century Fox, Universal Pictures, and Warner Bros. The MPAA promotes the interests of the Hollywood film industry to politicians in the federal government. The MPAA website provides many online resources, including fact sheets about copyright law as it pertains to the film industry and research reports that support its aims in policy lobbying.

Recording Industry Association of America (RIAA)
1025 F St. NW, 10th Fl., Washington, DC   20004
(202) 775-0101
website: www.riaa.com

The Recording Industry Association of America is a trade organization that represents the legal and financial interests of major music studios in the United States. The RIAA is particularly interested in protecting against copyright infringement and influencing policy to support the interests of its members. On its website, the RIAA publishes fact sheets to educate people about piracy, provides empirical data about sales, and also makes available many studies about the music industry and infringement.

US Copyright Office
101 Independence Ave. SE, Washington, DC   20559-6000
(877) 476-0778
website: www.copyright.gov

The US Copyright Office is the authority that oversees the application of copyright law in the United States. The Copyright Office collects and maintains information about registered copyrights, provides current and historical information about US copyright law, and advises the government on copyright policy. Its website provides registration forms, fact sheets, historical documents, annual reports, and brochures pertaining to copyright.

World Intellectual Property Organization (WIPO)
34, Chemin des Colombettes, CH-1211, Geneva   20
  Switzerland
+41 22 338 9111 • fax: +41 22 733 5428
website: www.wipo.int

Founded in 1967, the World Intellectual Property Organization is a United Nations agency dedicated to international
matters involving intellectual property, including treaties such
as the Berne Convention. WIPO provides economic analysis,
dispute resolution, and guidance in protecting intellectual
property and promoting creativity for its 185 member nations. WIPO publishes the *WIPO Magazine, Guide on Survey-
ing the Economic Contribution of the Copyright-Based Industries*, and *Collective Management of Copyright and Related
Rights.*

Bibliography of Books

Isabella Alexander *Copyright Law and the Public Interest in the Nineteenth Century.* Portland, OR: Hart, 2010.

Patricia Aufderheide and Peter Jaszi *Reclaiming Fair Use: How to Put Balance Back in Copyright.* Chicago: University of Chicago Press, 2011.

Lionel Bently, Jennifer Davis, and Jane C. Ginsberg, eds. *Copyright and Piracy: An Interdisciplinary Critique.* New York: Cambridge University Press, 2010.

Mario Biagioli, Peter Jaszi, and Martha Woodmansee *Making and Unmaking Intellectual Property: Creative Production in Legal and Cultural Perspective.* Chicago: University of Chicago Press, 2011.

Marcus Boon *In Praise of Copying.* Cambridge, MA: Harvard University Press, 2010.

James Boyle *The Public Domain: Enclosing the Commons of the Mind.* New Haven, CT: Yale University Press, 2010.

Jerry Brito *Copyright Unbalanced: From Incentive to Excess.* Arlington, VA: Mercatus Center at Georgetown University, 2012.

Alex Sayf Cummings *Democracy of Sound: Music Piracy and the Remaking of American Copyright in the Twentieth Century.* New York: Oxford University Press, 2013.

Peter Decherney	*Hollywood's Copyright Wars: From Edison to the Internet.* New York: Columbia University Press, 2012.
Stephen Fishman	*The Copyright Handbook: What Every Writer Needs to Know.* 11th ed. Berkeley, CA: Nolo, 2010.
Rebecca Giblin	*The Code Wars: 10 Years of P2P Software Litigation.* Northampton, MA: Edward Elgar, 2011.
James S. Heller, Paul Hellyer, and Benjamin J. Keele	*The Librarian's Copyright Companion.* 2nd ed. Buffalo, NY: Hein, 2012.
Bill D. Herman	*The Fight over Digital Rights: The Politics of Copyright and Technology.* New York: Cambridge University Press, 2013.
Renee Hobbs	*Copyright Clarity: How Fair Use Supports Digital Learning.* Newbury Park, CA: Corwin, 2010.
Monica Horten	*The Copyright Enforcement Enigma: Internet Politics and the 'Telecoms' Package.* Basingstoke, UK: Palgrave MacMillan, 2011.
Adrian Johns	*Piracy: The Intellectual Property Wars from Gutenberg to Gates.* Chicago: University of Chicago Press, 2011.
Joe Karaganis, ed.	*Media Piracy in Emerging Economies.* Brooklyn, NY: Social Science Research Council, 2011. Available from http://piracy.americanassembly.org.

Joe Karaganis and Lennart Renkema — *Copy Culture in the US & Germany.* New York: American Assembly, 2013. Available from http://piracy.americanassembly.org.

Robert Levine — *Free Ride: How Digital Parasites Are Destroying the Culture Business and How the Culture Business Can Fight Back.* New York: Doubleday, 2011.

Jason Mazzone — *Copyfraud and Other Abuses of Intellectual Property Law.* Stanford, CA: Stanford University Press, 2011.

Kembrew McLeod and Peter DiCola — *Creative License: The Culture and Law of Digital Sampling.* Durham, NC: Duke University Press, 2011.

Robert P. Merges — *Justifying Intellectual Property.* Cambridge, MA: Harvard University Press, 2011.

Ashley Packard — *Digital Media Law.* 2nd ed. New York: Wiley-Blackwell, 2012.

William Patry — *How to Fix Copyright.* New York: Oxford University Press, 2011.

Kal Raustiala and Christopher Sprigman — *The Knockoff Economy: How Imitation Sparks Innovation.* New York: Oxford University Press, 2012.

Aaron Schwabach — *Fan Fiction and Copyright: Outsider World and Intellectual Property Protection.* Burlington, VT: Ashgate, 2011.

John Tehranian	*Infringement Nation: Copyright 2.0 and You.* New York: Oxford University Press, 2011.
United States International Trade Commission	*China: Effects of Intellectual Property Infringement and Indigenous Innovation Policies on the US Economy: Investigation No. 332-519.* Washington, DC: US International Trade Commission, 2011.

Index

A

Actors' Equity Association (AEA), 67

Actual transfer distribution theory, 174–177

Adobe Systems
  DMCA legal challenges, 133
  e-book formatting, 131–132
  legitimization of P2P, 184–185

Advanced E-book Processor software, 127, 131

Agfa Monotype Corporation, 132–133

Amazon (company)
  best-selling textbook study, 61
  duplicate book accusations, 193
  e-book market monopolization, 79, 200–201
  first rights doctrine, 55
  infringement easements, 190–191, 193
  legal digital downloads, 79
  plagiarized book removal, 188
  vendor difficulties, 129

American Association of Independent Music (A2IM), 139, 140

American Federation of Labor-Congress of Industrial Organizations (AFL-CIO), 67

American Federation of Musicians (AFM), 67

American Federation of Television and Radio Artists (AFTRA), 67

American Guild of Musical Artists (AGMA), 67

American Society of Composers, Authors, and Publishers (ASCAP), 42, 109

Ammori, Marvin, 47–52

A&M Records Inc. v. Napster Inc. (2001), 104

Anti-bot software, 115, 117, 121, 123–124

Apple products, 47–52, 110, 133–134

Aragones, Maria Christine D., 33–42

Ars Technica (website), 89, 142–143

Assey, James, 138

Association of American Publishers, 20, 97

Atlantic Monthly (magazine), 169

Atlantic v. Anderson (1999), 31

Atomic Dog (Clinton), 38

AT&T, 140

Audio Home Recording Act (1992), 157

B

Baer, Harold, Jr., 20

BBC (British Broadcasting Corporation), 86

BearShare, 104

Beastie Boys, 39

Bengloff, Rich, 139

Biden, Joe, 29

BitTorrent
  changing of focus, 183

copyright litigation, 95, 180, 184

declining searches, 160

illegal downloading and, 85

legitimization transition, 184

liability protections, 180

mechanics of use, 172, 181

World of Warcraft updates, 185

Blackberry, licensed music streams, 110

Blizzard, anti-MDY Industries lawsuit, 115–118, 117, 120–125

Boing Boing, 16

Bono, Sonny, 15

Book copyright infringements, 60–61

The Bookseller (Page), 205

Boone v. Jackson (2007), 40

Bot software

Glider, 115–118, 121, 123–124

WoW Warden, 121

See also Anti-bot software

Box Office Mojo data, 76

Breaking Bad (TV series), 85

Bremmer, Ian, 154–155

Bridgeport Music, Inc. v. Dimension Films (2005), 40–41

Bridgeport v. UMG Recording Inc. (2008, 2009), 38

Brin, Sergey, 165–166

Broadcasting, Sound Recordings and Performance Artists Committee, 104

Broadcast Music Incorporated (BMI), 42, 109

Burnham, Brad, 162

Business Insider (website), 91

C

Cablevision Systems Corp., 140

Camara, Kiwi, 31

Capitol Records, 55–56

Capitol Records, Inc. v. Thomas (2008), 175–176

Capitol v. Foster (2004), 31

Capitol v. Redigi (2012), 55–56

CDs (compact discs)

burning/copying restrictions, 49

Copyright Act allowances, 54

copyright protections, 128–129

cost of theft per CD track, 31

ease in copying, 60

economic consequences of infringement, 71, 100–110, 172

non-infringement examples, 199

RIAA sales data, 101

Center for Copyright Information (CCI), 140, 142–143

Chamberlain Group, Inc. v. Skylink Technologies, Inc. (2004), 122–123, 125

Charlie's Diary (blog), 197

Charman-Anderson, Suw, 61–62

Choir (Newton), 39

Christin, Nicolas, 175

Clinton, Bill, 94

Clinton, George, 38

CNN.com, 61

Code Advisors (investment bank), 110

Coker, Mark, 188–189, 191–194

Comcast Corp., 140

Congressional Research Service, 15–16, 76, 79, 84

Content theft. *See* Online content theft

Copyleft movement, 147, 148, 198

Copyright Act (1976)
    breach-of-contract claims, 120
    claims for conversion, 25–26
    Congressional revision, 20–21
    description, 14, 24
    historical background, 178
    motivation for passage, 15
    music sampling statute, 35–37
    protected rights, 26
    publication, defined, 178
    RIAA claims data, 173
    Section 303 preemption, 25
    stated purpose, 113, 114
    See also Fair use doctrine; First-sale doctrine

Copyright Act (1978), 113

Copyright Alert System
    collaboration with ISPs, 136–138, 142–143
    consumers' services protections, 144
    illegal downloading notifications, 137
    non-prevention of copyright infringement, 141–146
    P2P sharing focus, 143–144
    prevention of copyright infringement, 135–136
    transparency concerns, 145–146

Copyright infringement
    defined as not theft, 28–32, 198–199
    defined as theft, 22–27
    distribution theories, 173–178, 180

e-books, ethical concerns, 195–201

employment consequences, 138–139

facilitation, by P2P companies, 171–181

music sale damages, 100–110

music sampling determination, 33–42

negative impact, 63–72

overstatement of negative impact, 73–82

physical possession issues, 25–26

self-published e-books and, 187–194

terms of use infringement, 118–119

willful vs. non-willful, 30

See also Economic costs of infringement; Infringers of copyrights

Copyright infringement litigation
    amicus brief filings, 97
    BitTorrent, 95, 180, 184
    copyright maximalists, 95–96
    economic impact, 93
    Google, 20
    Internet service providers, 89, 90–91, 95
    legal/financial burdens, 88–99
    new approach, 95
    pursuit of weak defendants, 93–94
    RIAA discontinuance, 173
    Righthaven experiment, 92–93
    Thomas-Rasset civil case, 29–32
    See also individual legal cases

Copyright laws
    adaptation to technologies, 202–211

automatic protections, 156–157

balancing protections, innovations, 158

core functions/purpose, 75–76, 107–108

economic importance, 203–204

format-neutral status, 205–206

holder of copyright rights, 65

obsolescence due to technology, 202–211

protections, 14

See also Fair use doctrine; *individual laws*

Copyright maximalists, 95–96

Copyright-protected CDs, 128–129

Copyright Term Extension Act (CTEA, 1998), 15, 113

Corporate copyright, 14

Costco v. Omega (2010), 51–52

Couts, Andrew, 49

Craigslist, 16, 49

Creative Commons (CC) licensing

copyleft movement and, 147, 148, 198

historical background, 148

intentions for musicians, 149

promotion of unknown artists, 150–151

use by artists, 150

visual guide, 217–218

D

Data mining, 211

Davis, Fred, 110

De minimis use, 34, 39–42

Department for Professional Employees (DPE), 63–72

Dibango, Manu, 35

Dickinson Wright (law firm), 90

Digital (online) economics, 79, 80–81

Digital e-readers, 60–61

Digital Millennium Copyright Act (DMCA)

anti-circumvention provisions, 134

Blizzard-MDY Industries lawsuit, 115–118, 120–125

blocking of streaming media recording, 132

bot violations, 121–122

copyright circumvention tool ban, 129

copyright infringement protections, 115–125

description, 15, 94, 127–128, 157

exemptions determination, 169

infringer penalties, 119

jeopardization of fair use doctrine, 126–133

new possibilities, 125

passage, 15

typeface tools challenges, 132–133

Digital rights management (DRM)

description, 60

DMCA protections, 15

e-books management and, 197

harm to fair use, 128–129

jailbreaking/rooting smartphones, 170

strict enforcement recommendation, 214

Digital Trends (website), 143

DMCA. *See* Digital Millennium Copyright Act

Dodd, Christopher, 23

Domain Name System, 74, 162–163

Donnelly, Michael, 116–118, 120–121

Dowling v. United States (1985), 23, 32

DPE (Department for Professional Employees, AFL-CIO), 63–72

Drudge Report (website), 89

Duncan, Geoff, 143

Dunlap, Thomas M., 96, 98

DVD Copy Control Association, 130, 157

DVD CopyWare, 129

DVDs (digital versatile discs)
customer copying inability, 133–134
DMCA blocking of legitimate copying, 129–130
owner rights, 54
RealDVD software and, 130

E

eBay, 48–51

e-books
Amazon market monopoly, 200–201
copy protections, 127
copyright infringement, encouragement of, 62, 187–194
copyright infringement, ethical concerns, 195–201
customer experience diminishment, 193–194
customer protections, 192
digital rights management, 197
distribution by Smashwords, 188–189, 191–194
economic factors, 62

fair use blocking by DMCA, 131–132
growing infringement, 60–61
infringement prevention, 61–62
quality-related content guidelines, 193
royalty-free content issues, 188–189
software, 127, 131

Economic costs of infringement
compensation losses, 65–66
costs of theft per CD track, 31–32
impact on US Gross Domestic Product, 66
legal/financial burdens, 88–99
lost sales, 60
negative impact, 63–72
royalty theft, 25
US GAO report, 69–70, 74–75

eDonkey, 104

Elcomsoft, 131

Electronic Frontier Foundation (EFF)
applications for exemptions, 130–131
cell phone protection concerns, 169
Copyright Alert Systems concerns, 145
fight against trolling threats, 95
PIPA bill proposal, 16
proposal for contacting legislators, 57

EMI Music North America, 140

The End of the Free Market (Bremmer), 154–155

End user license agreements, 56–57

Entertainment industries
   businesses and community
      support, 67, 69
   damages from piracy, 70–71
   importance to US economy,
      66–67
   live theatre piracy, 72
   See also Motion picture indus-
      try; Music piracy; Television
      industry
Entrepreneurial capitalism, 155
Essex, Mike, 187–194
European Court of Justice, 206,
   207, 208
Eve, Martin Paul, 195–201

F

*Facebook, Inc. v. Power Ventures,
   Inc.* (2009), 125
Fair use doctrine
   defined, 19, 127
   Google and, 20
   jeopardization by DMCA,
      126–134
   Righthaven and, 96–97
Federal Communications Commission (FCC), 102
File-sharing
   call for legalization, 109
   debate about response, 107
   defined as stealing, 29
   description, 101
   doubts about harmfulness,
      105–106
   economic impact, 108
   litigation against individuals,
      105
   monitoring by the RIAA, 142
   popularity, 102

recording industry legal victo-
   ries, 103–104
record sales impact, 106
See also Online piracy; Peer-
   to-peer (P2P) services; *individual companies*
First-sale doctrine, 47–52
   Apple product sales, 51
   California Ninth Circuit case,
      51–52
   Copyright Act application, 50
   Craigslist item sales, 48–49, 51
   description, 49, 54
   digital goods protections,
      53–57
   dislike of, by copyright own-
      ers, 55
   eBay item sales, 48–51
   licensing issues, 56–57
   New York federal court case,
      50
   sale of goods rule, 49–50
   US Supreme Court ruling,
      50–52
Football Association Premiere
   League (FAPL, UK), 207–208
Fortune (magazine), 215
Fragmental familiarity standard,
   38
Franken, Al, 163–164
*Free Ride: How Digital Parasites
   Are Destroying the Culture Busi-
   ness* (Levine), 96–97
Free Software Foundation, 57
Frisch, Matt, 61, 62

G

Gardner, Eriq, 88–99
Gates, Bill, 159
Geekette Marketing, 189

Gibson, Steven, 90–91, 96, 98

Gillibrand, Kirsten, 164

Glider (software), 115–118, 121, 123–124

Gnutella, 172

Gomez, Jeff, 205

Google
book content digitization, 20
duplicated content searches, 191
effect on content business, 89, 91, 99
pirated content focus, 119, 188
search engine features, 89, 119
vanity self-searches, 190
website blackout participation, 16

Google Maps, 51

Grand Upright Music, Ltd. v. Warner Bros. Records, Inc. (1991), 41–42

Grassley, Chuck, 164

Green, Stuart P., 30

Grokster, 94, 102–103, 104–105

H

HADOPI law (France), 146

Hand Clapping Song (Bug Music), 39–40

Hardawar, Devindra, 182–186

Hargreaves Review (2011 report), 207, 209, 211

HathiTrust, 20

Higgins, Parker, 145–146

Hollywood film industry
anti-VCR efforts, 157, 159
business model adaptations, 78
consumer media-consumption strategies, 159
political candidate contributions, 161
self-enrichment strategies, 155
support for SOPA/PIPA, 16, 92, 113–114, 162
See also Motion picture industry

The Hollywood Reporter (article), 95

Hotaling v. Church of Latter Day Saints (1997), 179–180

Howard, George, 148, 150, 151

How Creative Commons Can Stifle Artistic Output (Howard), 148–151

Howell, Beryl, 145

Howey, Hugh, 114

I

Illegal downloading
argument for legality, 109
BitTorrent use, 185
consequences, 186
Copyright Alert System notification, 137
non-labeling as theft, 30
P2P company liabilities, 104
possible benefits, 84–85, 199
US Supreme Court decision, 104

Independent Film & Television Alliance (IFTA), 139, 140

Information Assurance and Security Ethics in Complex Systems (Christin), 175

Infringers of copyrights
California civil laws and, 23
criminal trials, 31–32

DMCA penalties, 119, 125
economic consequences, 25,
  60
emotional impact, 32
establishment difficulties, 39
ineffectiveness of protections,
  15
lack of knowledge of consequences, 61
litigation involvement, 89
overseas infringers, 16
physical possession issues, 24,
  25
RIAA discontinuance of lawsuits, 173
royalty theft, 25
theft treatment benefits, 32
tools, 128
Institute for Policy Innovation,
  102, 172
Intellectual property
  copyrighted materials, 24, 65
  first-sale doctrine, 52
  IP Law Asia Summit, 23
  protection concerns, 34, 94
  theft consequences, 64, 71
  US GAO report, 60, 68, 69–70
  World Intellectual Property
    Organization, 66
*Intellectual Property: Observations
on Efforts to Quantify the Economic Effects of Counterfeit and
Pirated Goods* (US GAO report),
60, 68, 69–70
Intellectual Property Office (IPO,
UK), 203
International Alliance of Theatri-
cal Stage Employees, Moving
Picture Technicians, Artists and
Allied Crafts (IATSE), 67

International Brotherhood of
  Electrical Workers (IBEW), 67
International Federation of the
  Phonographic Industry (IFPI),
  71, 172
International Intellectual Property
  Alliance, 75
Internet
  copyrighted material data, 75
  copyright law decision and, 52
  copyright litigation, 89, 90–91,
    95
  digital distribution complica-
    tions, 79
  Domain Name System, 74,
    162–163
  economic impact, 153–155,
    165–166
  fair use and, 19–20
  file-sharing, 101, 109
  France's HADOPI law, 146
  freedom of expression and,
    204, 206
  infrastructure creation, 162
  lawful software downloads,
    207
  licensed music streams, 109–
    110, 132
  piracy tools, 128
  RIAA/music industry em-
    brace, 102
  stance against crony capital-
    ism, 165
  threats to traditional com-
    merce, 164–165
  US economy and, 154
  website blackout action, 16,
    163
Internet service providers (ISPs)
  content theft subscriber noti-
    fications, 136–137

Copyright Alert System collaboration, 136–138, 142–143
copyright infringement alerts, 144
encryption efforts, 143
infringement lawsuits, 95
large-scale piracy crackdown, 142
NCTA advisory role, 138
piracy and legal immunity, 163
six strike program, 142
See also Digital Millennium Copyright Act
iPad, 48, 50–51
iPhone, 110
iPod, 47, 133–134
iTunes, 79–80, 85, 129

J

Jackson, Michael, 35
Jacobsen v. Katzer (2008), 120
Jacobson, Jeffrey E., 103–104
Jailbreaking, of smartphones, 169–170
Jamaican toasting, 35
   See also Music sampling
Jean et al. v. Bug Music (2002), 39–40
Jobs, Steve, 165–166
John Wiley & Sons (publisher), 50, 53, 55, 95
Jones, Ben, 28–32

K

Karjala, Dennis, 15
Kaye, Laurence, 202–211
Kazaa, 94, 104, 172

Kemp, Jack, 154
Khanna, Derek S., 158, 169
Kindle e-book reader, 188, 193, 197, 200–201
Kirtsaeng, Supap, 50
Kirtsaeng v. John Wiley & Sons (2012, 2013), 50, 53, 55
Kohut, Mark, 196

L

Launching the Innovation Renaissance (Tabarrok), 159
Lee, Mike, 164
LeMay, Joey, 141–146
Lesser, Jill, 142–143, 144
Levine, Robert, 96–97
Librarian of Congress, 169–170
Licensed music streams, 109–110, 132
Limewire, 102, 104–105
Llewelyn, David, 23
Los Angeles Times (newspaper), 78
Lulu (company), 189–194

M

Making available distribution theory, 173, 177–178, 180
Marx, Karl, 198
Masnick, Michael, 160–161
Massively multiplayer online role-playing game (MMORPG), 116
McDonald, AJ, 189–190
McKinsey Global Institute, 154
McLuhan, Marshall, 205
McSherry, Corynne, 53–57
MDY Industries, LLC v. Blizzard Entertainment, Inc. (2009), 117–118, 120–125

Me and the Pirates Are Right
(Howey), 114

*Media Piracy in Emerging Econom-
ics* (Social Science Research
Council), 160

MGM Studios Inc. v. Grokster Ltd.
(2005), 104

Milch, Randal S., 139

Minnesota infringement law, 31

Mog, 107, 110

Moody, Glyn, 147–151

Motion Picture Association of
America (MPAA), 23, 138–139,
140, 161

Motion picture industry
Box Office Mojo data, 76
copyright infringements, 14
digital distribution, 56, 215
DMCA granting of veto
power, 157
downloading economics, 106
film professors exemption,
131
increasing content demands,
78
job creation, 67–68, 76
job losses, 138–139
negative piracy impact, 70,
71–72
piracy, 64, 77–80, 145
protections from public domain, 15
residual payments, 65–66
space-shifting, DVD to iPod,
134
trading over the Internet, 60
US economic impact, 64, 66,
69, 76
vendor payments, 69
See also Hollywood film industry

Mozilla, 16

Musical Instrumental Digital Interface (MIDI), 35

Music piracy
economic consequences, 71,
100–110, 172–173
origins of digital infringement, 60
record sales impact, 106
See also Recording industry;
Recording Industry Association of America

Music sampling
bright-line test, 42
Copyright Act statute, 35–37
copyright infringement determination, 33–42
defined, 34
de minimis use, 34, 39–42
fragmental familiarity standard, 38
Jamaican toasting origin, 35
substantial familiarity test,
37–38
three-second rule, 37

Music streams, licensed, 109–110,
132

N

Napster file-sharing company,
102–104, 185

National Cable & Telecommunications Association (NCTA), 138

Netflix, 79, 159–160

NetNames.com, 61

Neuburger, Jeffrey D., 115–125

Newton, James W., 39

Newton v. Diamond (2003), 39

New York Times (newspaper), 30,
91–92

The Next Great Copyright Act (Pallante), 14
Nielsen Soundscan, 76
Nijmeh, Ronnie, 188, 190, 192
No Electronic Theft Act (1997), 157
Noyes, Katherine, 149

O

Obama, Barack, 155, 158
Oberholzer-Gee, Felix, 76, 77, 106–108
Office and Professional Employees International Union (OPEIU), 67
O'Leary, Michael, 138
Online content theft
    consumers right to know, 138
    employment-related risk factors, 138–139
    independent producers and, 139
    ISP notifications to subscribers, 136–137
Online piracy
    basketball comparison, 84
    benefits, 85
    Biden, Joe, comments, 29
    economic consequences, 81
    historical background, 145
    innovative methods, 86–87
    The Pirate Bay website and, 79, 183–184
    political remedies, 81–82
    reasons for stopping, 83–87
    unwarranted hype, 74–75
    US Congress rhetoric, 75
    US GAO report, 60
    See also BitTorrent; File-sharing; Stop Online Piracy Act

Organization for Transformative Works, 130–131
Organization of Economic Co-operation Development (OECD), 68, 70

P

P2P. *See* Peer-to-peer (P2P) services
Page, Benedicte, 205
Page, Larry, 166
Pallante, Maria, 14, 113
Paramount Pictures Corporation, 140
Parloff, Roger, 215
Pass the Mic (Beastie Boys), 39
Patry, William, 175, 179
Peer-to-peer (P2P) services
    legal theories, 181
    possible legitimization, 182–186
    recording company settlements, 105
    software file sharing, 29, 104–105, 172
    usefulness, 185–186
    See also specific companies and services
Penenberg, Adam L., 190
Penguin (Google search) penalty, 119
Perrin, Chad, 212–219
Perry, SKS, 188, 190–191
Pink, Jonathan, 22–27
Piracy. *See* Music piracy; Online piracy; Stop Online Piracy Act
The Pirate Bay (website), 79, 183–184

Please Don't Stop the Music
(Rihanna), 35
Pogue, David, 196
Preventing Real Online Threats to
Economic Creativity and Theft
(PROTECT) of Intellectual Prop-
erty Act (PIPA), 16, 74, 84, 92,
113–114, 162
Prewitt, Jean, 139
Prioritizing Resources and Organi-
zation for Intellectual Property
Act (2008), 157
Private Label Rights content
(PLR), 188–194
Project Gutenberg, 189
Pynchon, Thomas, 196

R

Randazza, Marc, 96–97
RealDVD software, 130
RealNetworks, 130, 132
Recording industry
concert revenues data, 77
file-sharing damage, 102–104
litigation, 102–104
piracy-related employment
data, 71
revenue losses, 100
Recording Industry Association of
America (RIAA)
appeals to lawsuits, 30
CD sales data, 101
copyright definition, 107
fair use challenges and, 97
illegal file-sharing, economic
implications, 102
litigation actions, 31, 89, 94–
96, 172–173
monitoring of file-sharing
networks, 142

Thomas-Rasset, Jammie, court
case, 29–32
See also Copyright Alert System
Reddit, 16
Redigi, 54, 55–56
Reece, Vanessa, 182, 189–190
Reid, Harry, 164
RIAA. *See* Recording Industry Association of America
Righthaven
anger of lawyers, 95–96
financial burdens created by,
88–99
ignoring of fair use doctrine,
96–97
media-related agreements,
92–93
mysterious motivations, 98–99
public relations maelstrom,
90–91
Rooting, of smartphones, 169–170
Rubio, Marco, 164
Ruffini, Patrick, 152–166

S

Salam, Reihan, 152–166
Sanchez, Julian, 73–82
*SAS Institute Inc. v. World Pro-
gramming Ltd* (2013), 206
Schumer, Chuck, 164
Screen Actors Guild (SAG), 67,
164
Search Engine Land (Sullivan), 119
*Sebastian Int'l v. Consumer Prod-
ucts (PTY) Ltd.* (1988), 52
Security Is Sexy (blog), 54
Seidenberg, Steven, 100–110
Sherman, Cary, 138

Sklyarov, Dmitry, 131
Smartphones, 169–170
Smashwords, 188–189, 191–194
Smith, Lamar, 1621
Social Science Research Council, 160
Sonny Bono Copyright Term Extension Act (1998), 15, 156
Sony Music Entertainment, 140
Sony Pictures Entertainment Inc., 140, 142
Soul Makossa song (Dibango), 35
Space-shifting, 199–200, 210–211
Spotify, 79, 110, 184–185
Stallman, Richard, 149, 198
Starlight Runner Entertainment, 205
Stephens Media, 92–93, 98
Stop Online Piracy Act (SOPA)
    Congressional opposition, 163
    Congressional support, 162–163
    consideration by Congress, 84, 162–163
    description, 15–16
    economic harm claims, 74, 84–85
    grassroots activists conflicts, 153–154
    Hollywood film industry support, 16, 92, 113–114
    online piracy reduction efforts, 79, 92
    opposition battle, 16, 153–154, 163–166
    support, 96
Storm, Darlene, 54
Streambox, 132
Streamripper, 132
Stross, Charlie, 197
Substantial familiarity test, 37–38

Sullivan, Danny, 119
Supreme Court (US)
    first-sale doctrine case, 47–52
    infringement ruling, 23–24
    Sonny Bono Act defense, 156
    See also individual court cases

T

Tabarrok, Alex, 159
Tea Party Patriots, 163–164
Television industry
    piracy of shows, 65
    residual payments, 65–66
    US economic impact, 64
    vendor payments, 69
Thomas-Rasset, Jammie, 29–32
Three-second rule (music sampling), 37
Time Warner Cable, 95, 140
Toder, Brian, 31
TorrentFreak, 28–29
ToU (terms of use) infringement, 118–119
Treaties on the Functioning of the European Union (TFEU), 208
Tritton Technologies, 129
The True Cost of Copyright Industry Piracy to the US Economy (Institute for Policy Innovation), 102
Tumblr, 16
TuneCore (blog), 148
Twentieth Century Fox Film Corporation, 140
Twitter, 16

U

United Kingdom (UK)
    changes to copyright law, 209

copyright exception for libraries, 203
copyright infringement issue, 29
copyright law discussions, 206
corporate-tax-free e-book sales, 200
satellite broadcast rights, 207–208
United States
CD retail sales data, 101
copyright alert collaborations, 140, 142
copyright law protections, 14
counterfeiting/piracy threats, 75, 84, 143
entertainment industry employment, 161
entertainment industry unions, 67
entrepreneurial capitalism, 155
global economy revenues, 154
GM/Chrysler bailouts, 155
Google book-scanning project, 20
international treaty obligations, 178
labor unions, 67
personal entertainment spending data, 153–154
the White House, 145, 169
See also Economic costs of infringement; Supreme Court (US)
Universal City Studios LLC, 140
Universal Music Group Recordings, 140
Universal v. Reimerdes (2001), 129
UN World Intellectual Property Organization (WIPO), 66
US Bureau of Labor Statistics, 161

US Circuit Court of Appeals, 97, 104
US Congress
DMCA exemptions determination, 169, 170
extensions of copyright terms, 155–156
Internet infringement action, 75
off-shoring of business concerns, 55
opposition to SOPA, 163
PIPA consideration, 16, 74, 84, 92, 162
publication, defined, 178, 179
support for SOPA, 15–16, 79, 84, 162–163
See also Copyright Act
US Copyright Group, 95
US Copyright Office, 131
US Court of Appeals, 6th circuit, 40
US Department of Commerce, 66
US District Court (New York), 20
US Government Accountability Office (US GAO), 60, 68, 69–70, 74–75
US Immigration and Customs Enforcement, 158
US Justice Department, 92
US Ninth Circuit Court of Appeals, 51, 115–117, 120–121, 121–123, 125
US Register of Copyrights, 14, 113
US Senate Judiciary Committee, 29, 162
US Trade Representative, 70
UsedSoft GmbH v. Oracle International Corp (2012), 207

V

Verizon, 139, 140
Vernor v. Autodesk (2010), 117–118
Virtual Private Networks (VPN), 145
von Lohman, Fred, 126–133

W

Walt Disney Studios/Company, 15, 140, 142
Warner Bros. Entertainment Inc., 140
Warner Music Group, 140
Watt, Mel, 163
Wikipedia, 16, 189
Willful infringement, 30
Wordpress, 16
World Intellectual Property Organization (UN WIPO), 66
World of Warcraft, 116–118, 120–121, 123–124, 182, 185
WoW Warden, 115, 117, 121, 123–124
Writers Guild of America, East (WGAE), 67

Y

Yglesias, Matthew, 83–87

Z

Zimmerman, Kollin J., 171–181
Zuckerberg, Mark, 165–166